S0-AKB-388

q355.14 Company of
C737m   Military
c.2   Historians
v.1   Military
         uniforms in
         America

CFD 7/94 ⑤

MITCHELL PARK BRANCH

Palo Alto City Library

The individual borrower is responsible for all library material borrowed on his card.

Charges as determined by the CITY OF PALO ALTO will be assessed for each overdue item.

Damaged or non-returned property will be billed to the individual borrower by the CITY OF PALO ALTO.

21M 5/74

MILITARY UNIFORMS IN AMERICA

The Era of the American Revolution

1755-1795

The Seal of the Company of Military Historians commemorates the founding of the United States Army. On June 14, 1776, the Continental Congress resolved "That six companies of expert riflemen be immediately raised in Pennsylvania, two in Maryland, and two in Virginia. These "... remarkably stout and hardy men, many of them exceeding six feet in height, clad in hunting shirts and armed with a rifle-barreled gun, a tomahawk ... and a long knife ..." were the first United States Regulars.

MILITARY UNIFORMS IN AMERICA

The Era of the American Revolution

1755-1795

from the Series Produced by

THE COMPANY OF MILITARY HISTORIANS

John R. Elting
Colonel, US Army, Retired
Editor

Presidio Press

San Rafael, California, 1974

Library of Congress Catalog Card Number 74-21513

Copyright 1974 by the Company of Military Historians

ALL RIGHTS RESERVED

No material in this book may be used without the written permission of the publisher
or of the copyright owner.

Printed in the United States of America by E. A. John-
son Company, Roger Williams Press, East Providence,
Rhode Island. Color Separation plates by The Mowbray
Company, Providence, Rhode Island.

Introduction

IN 1882 the Marquis de Rochambeau, lately returned to France from representing his illustrious namesake at the Centennial Celebration at Yorktown, sent his aide out to buy books showing the uniforms of the American units which had participated in those ceremonies. When his aide returned empty-handed he was nonplussed. Perhaps the French booksellers were at fault? He wrote forthwith to the Quartermaster General of the U.S. Army in Washington. Perhaps he would send him the books?

This put the Quartermaster General in a quandary. There were no books. The great historical survey illustrated by H. A. Ogden had yet to appear, while the last illustrated uniform regulations — those of 1872 — were long out of date as well as out of print. How could he oblige the Marquis?

Feverishly, dispatches were sent to the Adjutants General of every state represented at the Yorktown Centennial, and to the Governors as well. Meanwhile officers of the Regular Army, from generals to A.D.C.'s, were marched off in full regalia to photographers in Washington, Baltimore, Detroit, and San Francisco, while whole troop units were mustered at their far-flung stations to face the camera. An artist, whose nearly illegible signature seems to be "Charles W. Larned," was commissioned to prepare a series of watercolors showing the uniform of each branch. In addition, helmets and insignia were carefully photographed on separate plates. All documents were neatly captioned in French in a fine copperplate hand.

The response from the states was varied. Some sent photographic portraits of their militia staffs. Others dressed up their whole Yorktown contingents and sent them to the local studios to be recorded. Others hired artists — or possibly importuned talented wives — to color the photographs to make them more lifelike. The Superintendent of the Virginia Military Institute sent actual swatches of cloth, both grey and scarlet, and samples of lace to evoke the dress of his cadets. Some Governors were content to provide mere watercolor sketches of their state flag.

When the compilation was complete, it filled two elephant folio albums which were dispatched to Paris in April, 1882, just six months after the ceremonies at Yorktown. These are at present in Providence, R. I., the property of Brown University.

Now just suppose that the Marquis de Rochambeau had requested illustrations of the uniforms worn at Yorktown in 1781 rather than 1881? Not the whole apparatus of Government, Federal and State, could have complied. This brings us to what the French would call the *raison d'etre* — literally the "reason for being" — of the present volume.

Our knowledge of the dress worn by our troops in the field at the most crucial moments leading to our nation's birth — first during the struggle to maintain an existence on this continent, then to gain our independence from England, was extremely meager before the present century. The dress of the Continental Army, though specified from time to time under general orders by the Commander in Chief, was rarely worn, if we can believe the written memoirs of combatants or the graphic sketches sent home by eyewitnesses, both allies and enemies.

It is enough to compare the prints by Johann Martin Will, published in Augsburg, c. 1777, from sketches "by a Bayreuth officer . . . in English service," or the "Real American Rifleman," published in the Hibernian Magazine in 1776, or the watercolor drawings made by Lieutenant J. B. deVerger of the French Deux-ponts Regiment during the Yorktown Campaign, with the chromolithographs of Ogden in *The Army of the United States*, first published by the Quartermaster General in 1885. The state of our knowledge at that time required Ogden to "go by the book" — or rather Washington's General Orders — so far as facing colors and insignia went, but he had to guess at the cut and style of the uniforms themselves, having nothing to go by but portraits of generals painted by Gilbert Stuart, Charles Willson Peale, John Trumbull, and other famous artists of the day, which were often not even contemporary. For example, there exists today portraits of Washington in Gilbert

Stuart's studio, now a museum, wearing the fall-down collar introduced during the French Revolution, which Stuart signed and had the temerity to date as 1776 or 1777, evidently to please some client. Consequently, poor Ogden put the whole Continental Army into the French collar, which was not generally worn before the 1790's. Only C. W. Peale seems to have consistently painted Washington in the narrow, flat, buttoned-down collar that he undoubtedly wore throughout the war.*

Although as early as 1877 Asa Bird Gardner had written a learned article on the subject in the *Magazine of American History,*** no serious illustrations of the dress of the American soldier in the Revolutionary War were published until Lieutenant Charles M. Lefferts of the 7th Regiment, New York National Guard, an amateur artist of considerable talent, compiled his comprehensive work, *Uniforms of the American, British, French and German Armies in the War of the American Revolution*, with fifty colored plates. Shortly after his death this was published by the New York Historical Society during the Sesquicentennial celebration of 1926. By a diligent search of the orderly books, memoirs, deserter descriptions in the contemporary press, state archives, and the journals of the Continental Congress, Lefferts succeeded in conveying to his fellow countrymen some idea of what the Continental soldier actually wore from 1775 to 1783, rather than what he was ordered to wear.

Curiously enough, though a number of illustrated books on uniforms had appeared in England, France, and Germany during the 18th Century, no one had taken the trouble to record the outlandish variations in military dress the English were obliged to adopt when fighting Indians, or even their Colonial cousins, in the wilds of North America. The private soldier was never a favorite subject of British military artists of that epoch; in fact, except for the designer of the "Cloathing Book" of 1742 and the paintings of David Morier in the 1750's and 1760's, I cannot think of any artist who portrayed the rank and file. As for the officers, their dearest wish when home on leave was to forget their bizarre garments worn on campaign, don their finest regimentals, and be painted by Gainsborough or Reynolds.

Lefferts did not try to portray the campaign dress of our enemies or our allies, not having the materials at hand, but followed the published works. Nor did he concern himself with military dress before or after the Revolution.

It was not until 1949, when the Company of Military Collectors and Historians was formed in Washington, D.C. by a small group of professional and amateur military scholars and collectors, that large gaps in our knowledge of military dress on this continent began to be filled.

The basic goal of the Company from its inception was to pool and disseminate knowledge of our military heritage, first by recruiting serious students in various fields, such as uniforms and insignia, weapons and accoutrements, military history and archaeology, tactics and drill, art, music, flags and heraldry, and weld them into a band of connoisseurs capable of producing an illustrated quarterly journal, supplemented by a series of carefully researched hand-colored plates showing the military dress worn on this continent from its discovery by Columbus to the present day. This program, incidentally, was to be implemented by volunteers.

Needless to say, the founders were all young, energetic, and optimistic. For this reason alone, the program as outlined above has been faithfully carried out during the past twenty five years, during which 100 issues of the Journal have been published, as well as over 400 colored plates of the *Military Uniforms in America* series, plus a series of phonograph records of authentic military music covering four wars.

Meanwhile, the membership — all formally proposed, seconded, and duly elected — has increased from 100 to over 2000, representing all fifty states, the District of Columbia, and twenty-seven foreign countries. Institutions subscribing to Company publications number over 200 libraries, universities, schools, learned societies and professional organizations.

To celebrate the coming-of-age of the Company of Military Historians, as it is now known, as well as our nation's Bicentennial, the Company has compiled and edited this present volume as its first offering to the general public.

In selecting the plates, we have chosen representative participants in the drama lasting half a century

*The only mention of a "standing cape" (fall-down collar) made during the Revolution appears in dress regulations for the Corps of Artillery in 1777 (*Magazine of American History*, Vol. I, No. 8, p. 473).
**Ibid. pp. 461-492.

that ultimately brought our nation to birth. During the French and Indian War this continent was occupied by three European powers: England, France, and Spain. Our principal enemy in this war, the French, became our principal ally in the next, while our day of reckoning with Spain, an ally during our War of Independence, did not occur for another half-century. Because of the peripheral, though nonetheless valuable, nature of the Spanish operations during the war, this volume is confined to English, American, French, and German troops who bore the brunt of the fighting from 1740 on.

It must be emphasized that the uniform plates issued by the Company were never intended to be works of art, but rather historical documents designed to portray with the greatest possible accuracy the types of men who fought on this continent in the military dress they actually wore, with the weapons and accoutrements with which they were equipped at each epoch and locale. The fact that many, if not most, of these troops had never before been depicted with this aim in view, presented problems of heroic proportions to the artists, as well as demanding much arduous research from the authors of the texts and the editors of the plate series.

Furthermore, due to the small issues involved (never more than 750 plates were printed) the only economically available process of reproduction required the artists to make line drawings in India ink, which were printed and sent with color notes to be colored by the stencil process. Meanwhile an editorial board, including the artist and authors of the descriptive texts, had to check the plates and correct proofs. In later years it became necessary to have the coloring done in Paris, due to rising prices and declining skills in the United States. The complications and labors involved in the above procedure cannot be overstressed, making heroes of the Plate Editors, from Frederick P. Todd, the first, to Captain James C. Tily, USN, Ret., who served until 1972 when relieved by Colonel John R. Elting. But it also put the artists into a form of a straight-jacket, as anyone can see by comparing the plates in this volume by the Company's principal artist, H. Charles McBarron, with his superb series, *The American Soldier 1775-1965* (issued from 1964 to 1969 in four-color reproduction by the Office of the Chief of Military History, Department of the Army), which faithfully reproduces every nuance of this fine artist's original paintings.

In addition to the exigencies of line and stencil work, the artist was often required to portray articles of dress never beheld by anyone now living and, in some cases, never illustrated before, even by a contemporary observer.

Anyone who has ever struggled with verbal descriptions of military dress, whether explicit, as in official uniform regulations, or vague, as in eyewitness accounts of troops on the march or in combat, knows how difficult this can be. The nomenclature changes with the years — as every woman knows who still calls a once unmentionable garment by the French name *brassière* (now shortened in America to "bra"), whereas if she requests this object in a French shop today she will be shown an infant's sweater which crosses over the chest, since the current French term is *soutien-gorge*. Hence, the 18th Century "cape" in England is today's "collar" in America, whereas today's "cape" in America was a "cloak" in England; hence, English "lace" is American "braid," and what was once a "round hat" has become a "top hat."

McBarron, however, left as little as possible to chance. Whenever he got hold of a contemporary uniform coat or waistcoat, or even a pair of breeches, he simply took them apart and studied the seams, tried them on for fit, inspected the buttonholes, cuffs, measured the coattails along the calf of the leg, the lapels to see where they began and ended, then unbuttoned and rebuttoned them across the chest to see the effect when closed. This attention to detail is what goes to make a first-class military artist, together with an eye for color and a masterful brush, pen, or pencil.

McBarron, steeped in the artistic traditions of his ancestral Scotland, is above all a "stylish" artist, very much in the manner of the late Reginald Wymer, also a Scot, whose gouache and watercolor drawings of British uniforms during the late 19th and early 20th Centuries stand out like swans in a flock of crows engulfed in the miserable swamp of chromolithography. However, with his keen historical sense and his passion for accuracy, McBarron succeeds in making the Indian-fighting troops of the 18th Century look quite tough when they were tough, and the ragged Continentals as destitute as they actually were during the miserable winter at Valley Forge.

Lending contrast to the series is the work of Peter Copeland, a very competent artist who prefers to stress the homespun character of the Continental soldier and leave the elegance to McBarron. His "Brother Jonathan" series, published from 1962 to 1968 in collaboration with Donald Holst, is both instructive and well researched, though it is evident that Copeland rarely envisages an American military man as particularly "spruce"; however, neither did many contemporary observers! His series *America's Fighting Man*, published in collaboration with Harold Peterson in New York in 1971, can be justly termed a collection of caricatures.

Frederic E. Ray, Jr. is probably, next to McBarron, the most classic artist represented in this collection. A distinguised and prolific historical artist and illustrator, familiar with all periods, he is known chiefly through his illustrated brochures, *Fort Ticonderoga* (1950), *Fort McHenry and the Star-Spangled Banner* (1959), *Story of the Alamo* (1955), *Gettysburg Sketches* (c. 1960), *Uniforms of the Union*, and *Uniforms of the Confederacy* (1960), and as editor of *O! Say Can You See, The Story of America Through Great Painting* (1970).

Clyde Risley, a fine artist, has produced a handsome series of Revolutionary uniform prints issued by K/S Historical Publications in Saddle River, N. J. from 1966 to 1969, in large and small folios, as well as postcard size.

Frederick T. Chapman is chiefly known through his illustrations in many books, including *Cadet Grey* by Frederick P. Todd, of whom more anon, published in New York in 1955.

To ensure authenticity in the dress and accoutrements of foreign contingents who fought in America, the Company has been fortunate in obtaining copious advice from the late Cecil C. P. Lawson, dean of British uniform authorities, ever since the first volume of his five-volume work *History of the Uniforms of the British Army* appeared in 1940 and terminated only at his death in 1967.

Herbert Knötel, the dean of German military artists, in 1918, who at an early age completed the *"grosse" Uniformenkunde* of his famous father, Professor Richard Knötel, has happily supplied all the plates of the German units who participated in the Revolutionary War as British mercenaries. Knötel continued his father's work throughout his own lifetime, producing the now famous *Handbuch der Uniformkunde*, first published in Hamburg in 1937 and republished many times since. Co-editor with Hans Brauer of the *Uniformenbogen and Fahnentafeln* from 1926 to 1932, and the *Uniformenkunde, Neue Folge* from 1936 to 1939, he continued after the war until his death in 1963 to illustrate the majority of books published in Germany on uniforms, military history, or regimental records. As an authority on all questions of European military dress and equipment of whatever epoch, he has received world-wide recognition.

Since World War II Eugène Lelièpvre has been a prolific illustrator of books on French military dress, beginning with Commandant Bucquoy's *Fanfares et Musiques des Troupes à Cheval* in 1943. Since then he has published *Cavaliers du Roy Soleil* in 1945, *Au Service de la France. Trois Siecles d'Histoire Militaire*, published in Baden-Baden in 1947, and *Nos Derniers Cavaliers. Le 7e Groupe de Spahis Algeriens* in 1949, as well as several series of military costume plates showing French troops in Canada 1755-1760, in the First and Second Empires, and in World War I. Some of these, together with colored plates of historic American, British, French, and Italian uniforms from the 18th Century on have been published in Bala-Cynwyd, Pa., by Captain James C. Tily during the last decade.

Among the American artists represented in this collection, Eric I. Manders deserves special mention as a prolific and valuable contributor to the Company publications in both drawings and research. Philip N. Katcher, a professional editor and photographer in Philadelphia, and James T. ("Tom") Jones, a military artist from Texas, have lately joined our corps of contributing artists with most promising results while Russel Gammage of London, a military artist and model soldier-maker, and Dennis Martin, a professional illustrator in neighoring Ontario, have joined our distinguised corps of foreign artists.

Though the undersigned has written several books and a number of magazine articles, she has never dared write a text for an MUIA plate. This can be a traumatic experience. Experts fairly come out of the walls to question your assumptions on this, that, and the other detail. If the form of the headdress is substantially correct, the plume is wrong — it should be a tuft; if the cartouche box is right, the belt-plate is wrong — it should be oval. Weaponry is a real trap for those who jump when a piece goes off. Therefore, the authors of the texts published in this volume have my sympathetic admiration.

First to be mentioned among them is Frederick P. Todd, late Colonel of the A.U.S., former director of the West Point Museum, alumnus (like Lefferts) of Co. K, 7th Regt., NYNG, author of many books in and out of print, and one in the press — the first of five volumes entitled *American Military Equipage 1851-1872*. It is hoped that this will be published serially under the sponsorship of the Company, of which he is a founder and has served variously as President, Editor-in-Chief, and Plate Editor, and as Governor throughout its existence. In addition, he has served as historical consultant to myriad organizations and individuals.

Next comes Colonel John R. Elting, late Associate Professor of Military Art at the United States Military Academy, co-author of the monumental West Point *Military History and Atlas of the Napoleonic Wars*, published in New York in 1964, Governor of the Company and Plate Editor, now Vice President and editor of this book. Both Colonels Todd and Elting are distinguised collectors as well as producing scholars.

Other texts have been co-authored by several of the artists mentioned above. In addition, the authors include: René Chartrand, Military Curator of National Historic Sites in Canada; Marco Zlatich, erstwhile librarian and Governor of the Company; the late James P. Simpson, military scholar and collector, and member of the celebrated Essex Troop, NJNG; Dr. George A. Snook, Company Governor and authority on early American military history; Detmar Finke, a founder of the Company, professional historian in the Department of the Army's Office of the Chief of Military History; Tom Parker, military artist and former Governor of the Company; Henry I. Shaw, Jr., Chief Historian of the U.S. Marine Corps, Company Governor and former Editor-in-Chief; Colonel Arthur P. Wade, U.S. Army historian; Cap-

. tain Rutledge F. Smith, USNR, Ret., collector and authority on the Navy Medical Corps; Captain Fitzhugh McMaster, USN, Ret., authority on the military history of South Carolina; F. Donald Holst, Museum Display Technician at the Smithsonian Institution, collaborator with Clyde Risley in the series of Revolutionary uniform plates published by K/S Historical Publications, 1964-1969; Major Donald M. Londahl-Smidt, USAFR, specialist in uniforms of the Revolutionary War; and the late Marcel Baldet for many years Secretary of the celebrated French *Societé de la Sabretache*, author of *Figurines et Soldats de Plomb*, Paris, 1961, and *La Vie Quotidienne dans les Armées de Napoléon*, Paris, 1964.

It is to be noted that the plates in this volume have been reprinted from their original black outline-and-stencil format in a modern four-color process, and that the original size has been slightly reduced to make the volume more convenient to handle. Andrew Mowbray has been in charge of designing the book and supervising all typography and color work and has taken great pains to reproduce the original MUIA plates as faithfully as possible.

The Company of Military Historians hopes that this, their first public offering, representing the unselfish labors of many talented and dedicated men over the past 25 years, will give pleasure and inspiration to those Americans who are neither ashamed of our nation's past nor unduly fearful of its future. For, in the words of the late Robert Ingersoll, "Despite what the Evolutionists tell us about where we came from and what the Revolutionists tell us about where we're going to, the fact remains that we are *here*." Thanks, I may add, to many of the soldiers portrayed in this book.

Anne S. K. Brown

Providence, R. I.
May, 1974

Preface

IN the twenty-five years since the *Military Uniforms in America* series was initiated by the Company of Military Historians, over 400 separate units have been portrayed and described. Nearly ninety of these relate to the era of the American Revolution. From these, the editors have selected 60 plates which in their opinion best represent the military forces of the period. In preparing the texts and illustrations for publication, the editors have updated and corrected the written descriptions, using additional factual information found after the original versions were published. Errors or omissions in the original illustrations have also been corrected. The end product — this book — thus presents an authentic, accurate, and factual description of the units depicted.

Although primary emphasis has been placed upon the Revolutionary War years, the editors felt it necessary to include both the French and Indian Wars and the post-Revolutionary War era. This encourages the reader to compare changes in both uniforms and equipment during the three major time periods as well as readily illustrating the improvement and changes in items of military gear.

This work is not intended as a definitive portrayal of all forces of this era. It is instead a selective description of typical military units of the various nations military which participated in the conflicts in North America during the latter half of the eighteenth century. British, French, German, Provincial, and American units are all represented.

Arrangement of units within each major category has been made by national grouping. British regulars are listed in regimental numerical sequence; French and German units, alphabetically. Provincial units and units from the various states are similarly arranged. Continental Line units are alphabetically listed by state and numerically within each state listing. Dates included with the title of each illustration indicate the approximate time when the uniforms portrayed were worn by that unit.

The major research for this volume represents the work of the many artists and authors who worked on the illustration and text for each of the units included herein. To provide well-deserved recognition, we have listed first the artist and then the author or authors immediately following the text for each illustration.

Footnotes for some of the French and German texts do not follow our normal format and may even appear incomplete. These have been retained purposely in the form prepared by Eugène Lelièpvre and Herbert Knötel. As such they are an indication of scholarly research accomplished in the manner of outstanding French and German historians.

In addition to the many references cited by the artists and authors, three relatively recent works have been of inestimable value to the editors. These are: Frederick Anderson Berg's *Encyclopedia of the Continental Army* and Harold L. Peterson's *Arms and Armor in Colonial America, 1526-1783* and *The Book of the Continental Soldier*.

No effort such as this can represent the work of one man. Many other Company members have assisted in preparing the plates for publication. Company Founder and Fellow Mrs. Anne S. K. Brown graciously consented to write the Introduction. Company President George S. Pappas has supervised the overall preparation, assisted in the editing, and coordinated production. Our Treasurer Andrew Mowbray has served as our professional and technical coordinator and as liaison with the publisher. Mrs. Elizabeth V. Hassler assisted in many editorial tasks including the thankless work of verifying details and citations. Advice and assistance has been given by other Company members including Fred Berg, Harold Peterson, and Gordon Chappell. Typing of this manuscript was done by Mrs. Linda Brenneman and Mrs. Judy Meck. Special thanks is also due the staffs of Presidio Press, the Mowbray Company, and the E. A. Johnson Company, Roger Williams Press, for their technical and professional assistance and advice. More than thanks and appreciation are due the families of all of us who needed so much their sympathetic understanding and endurance of our work in the preparation of this book.

J. R. E.

The illustrations and texts which follow represent the work of many members of the Company of Military Historians. Their voluntary research and study have enabled the Company to sponsor the *Military Uniforms in America* series for more than twenty-five years. Contributors to this volume include:

ARTISTS

Frederick T. Chapman
Peter F. Copeland
Russell Gammage
Tom Jones
Herbert Knötel
Eugene Leliepvre
H. Charles McBarron, Jr.
Eric I. Manders
Dennis Martin
Frederick E. Ray, Jr.
Clyde A. Risley

AUTHORS

Marcel Baldet
René Chartrand
John R. Elting
Detmar H. Finke
Russell Gammage
Donald W. Holst
Philip R. N. Katcher
Herbert Knötel
Donald M. Londahl-Smith
H. Charles McBarron, Jr.
Marko Zlatich

Fitzhugh McMaster
Eric I. Manders
George S. Pappas
Tom Parker
Henry I. Shaw, Jr.
James P. Simpson
Rutledge F. Smith
George A. Snook
Frederick P. Todd
Arthur P. Wade

Table of Contents

THE FRENCH AND INDIAN WARS, 1755-1770

British Regular Units

British Provincial Units

French Units

42nd (Royal Highland) Regiment of Foot, 1759-1763

This most celebrated of regiments saw its first service in America during the years 1756-1767. It won particular distinction for its desperate though unsuccessful attacks at Fort Ticonderoga in 1758 and its service at Havana in 1762. Probably its greatest fight was Bushy Run, 1763, where, although weak from the fevers of the West Indies and from hard marching, the Scots under Colonel Henry Bouquet smashed an Indian ambush and gave a bloody check to Pontiac's Rebellion.

When it arrived in North America, the Regiment wore Highland dress — short red jackets trimmed with regimental lace;[1] red waistcoats, blue bonnets, belted plaids of "Government Tartan"; and red-and-white checkered or striped hose. Cuffs and collars were buff. Grenadiers wore bearskin caps with a red flap edged with white and bearing the initials "GR" in white below a white crown.[2] Officers wore gold lace; sergeants, silver. Belts were made of black leather. The sporran (purse), made of plain buff leather with long tassels, probably was worn only for parade or off-duty. The sporrans shown in this plate are modeled after a fragment unearthed at Fort Ticonderoga.[3]

On July 3, 1758, King George II conferred the title "Royal" on the Regiment. This honor was not, as often stated, given as a reward for its courage at Ticonderoga for that battle was fought five days later. In keeping with this distinction, the Regiment's facings were changed from buff to blue.

The order books of the 42nd Regiment have much to say of its dress in North America. Officers in 1760 apparently received laced "regimental" coats, as illustrated in this plate, though they still retained the old-style jacket for regular wear. In 1761, white waistcoats are mentioned for wear on ceremonial occasions. The "belted plaid" — a combined kilt and shoulder plaid, all in one piece — proved unsuited to American campaigning and was generally used only for full-dress reviews and guard mount. The *Feilidh beag* or "little kilt" replaced it for general service.

The "Government Tartan", now popularly known as the "Black Watch" tartan, was considerably lighter than its modern version and contained light greens and bluish-greys. The Grenadier Company had a distinctive red stripe on its belted plaid as well as in its *Feilidh beag*. According to some sources this red stripe was used by the entire regiment for full dress. The exact facts concerning the red stripe, however, are not fully documented.

Officers wore linen breeches and boots for duty and the kilt for full dress. The "little kilt" was the normal service dress for enlisted men although during 1758-1760 short canvas breeches or "drawers" were worn with blue leggings for boat work and fatique details. In 1761, the "little kilt" replaced the breeches and was sometimes worn with leggings. During hot weather, coats might be worn without wasitcoats for drill and guard duty. Waistcoats and the "little kilt" were worn for service in the field. Checkered shirts were preferred for field service since they did not show dirt. Hair was cut to a uniform length ". . . allowing 10 inches below the tying, 8 inches of which is to be tied with ribbon and 2 inches at the end to be formed into a curl." Hair was powdered for ceremonies. A strip of the ". . . blackest bearskin that can be procurred . . . not to exceed 5 inches in length . . ." was worn on the bonnet. Sporrans are not mentioned and may have been discarded.[4]

Highland troops were issued muskets, bayonets, and broadswords. In addition, some men carried dirks and pistols. Officers and sergeants are described as using dirks instead of bayonets. There are records of payments on March 14 and November 24, 1759, to blacksmiths ". . . for cutting short the arms of the 42nd Regiment, by General Abercrombie's order, June 9, 1758."[5] This probably reduced the barrel length to forty-two inches. Sergeants carried halberds on parade, but commonly replaced them with muskets for campaigning. The light infantry company was issued "tomihawks", powder horns, and shot bags. Officers had fusees.

Within the Regiment, there was apparently considerable variation in dress and weapons, especially after the newly-raised 2nd Battalion arrived in America in late 1759. That battalion wintered in Albany while the 1st Battalion was scattered in six separate posts from Albany north to Halfway Brook. Such service did not encourage uniformity in either dress or weapons.

Fred Ray, Jr.
Frederick P. Todd
John R. Elting

[1]This lace was white with two red lines in 1751; white with one red line in 1768.

[2]The grenadier corporal in this plate is based on an official painting, now in Windsor Castle, by David Morier. The loops of white cord on his right shoulder indicate his grade.

[3]W.Y. Carman. *British Military Uniforms from Contemporary Pictures.* London: Spring Books, 1957. pp. 99-100. Officers of Highland regiments wore their sashes over the left shoulder so that the ends would not become entangled with the sword belt; J. Telfer Dunbar. *History of Highland Dress.* Edinburgh: Oliver & B., 1962. pp. 178-179; A. E. Haswell Miller. "A'n Early Portrait of a Highland Officer." *Journal of the Society of Army Historical Research.* Vol. 19, Autumn 1940. pp. 125-126 and comments on the article in *Journal . . .* Vol. 19, Winter 1940. p. 243.

[4]Dunbar, *Ibid.* pp. 180-181. In 1761 officers were to have black feathers instead of bearskin.

[5]Harold L. Peterson. *Arms and Armor in Colonial America, 1526-1783.* Harrisburg: Stackpole, 1956. pp. 167, 210-211.

Private in 'little kilt'

Grenadier Corporal

F. RAY -

Sergeant and Officer, Battalion Companies

42nd (Royal Highland) Regiment of Foot, 1759-1763

55th Regiment of Foot, 1758

Among the minor legends of early North America is that of Brigadier General Lord George Augustus Viscount Howe, killed in action near Fort Ticonderoga, July 6, 1758. An officer of energy, courgage, and common sense, he had accompanied Robert Rogers into the field to study ranger tactics and equipment, and had made himself beloved by regulars and provincials alike.

However, the description of him recorded by Anne MacVickers — who, as a young girl, had seen him at the Schuyler home — came to be considered somewhat idealized and over-drawn.

> . . . but Lord Howe always lay . . . with the regiment which he commanded [the 55th] and which he modelled in such a manner that they were ever after considered as an example to the whole American army . . . He forbade all displays of gold and scarlet . . . and set the example of wearing himself an ammunition [issue] coat . . . one of the surplus soldier's coats cut short . . . he ordered the muskets to be shortened . . . the barrels of their guns were all blackened . . . he set the example of wearing leggins . . . Lord Howe's [hair] was fine and very abundant; he, however, cropped it, and ordered everyone else to do the same.

In fact, Anne's description erred on the mild side. Richard Huck, Lord Loudoun's former surgeon, who served on the frontier for several years, wrote bluntly from Albany on May 29, 1758:

> The Art of War is much changed and improved here. I suppose by the end of summer it will have undergone a total Revolution. We are now literally an army of round Heads. Our hair is about an inch long; the Flaps of our Hats, which are wore slouched, about two inches and a half broad. Our Coats are docked rather shorter than the Highlanders, determined, Napier says, that the French shall not [illegible] in our Shirts. The Highlanders have put on Breeches and Lord Howe's Filabegs. Some from an affection to their Gorgets still wear them. Swords and Sashes are degraded, and many have taken up the Hatchet and wear Tomahawks.

An unidentified British officer agreed with Huck:

> You would laugh to see the droll figure we all cut. Regulars and Provincials are ordered to cut the brims of their hats off. The Regulars as well as the Provincials have left off their proper regimentals, that is, they have cut their coats so as to scarcely reach their waist. You would not distinguish us from common plough men.[2]

Fellow Robert E. Mulligan provided unexpected confirmation from the copybook of an unsuccessful trader named John McComb, which he found in the Albany archives. McComb, the father, incidentally, of Major General Alexander McComb who gained fame at Plattsburg in 1814, wrote on April 22, 1758 ". . . There certainly will be a great demand for close by the time the Army returns to Winter quarters, as they have cut all their Coats short, which will render them useless for the Winter."

> Every effort apparently was made to fit the men for woods fighting: . . . 10 Rifled Barrelled Guns were delivered out to each regiment to be put into the hands of their best Marksmen . . . in every man's knapsack were to be thirty pounds of meal, which he was expected to cook for himself . . . Whenever the men march they are to put their provisions in their haversacks and roll them up in their blankets like the Rangers . . . and all Troops under Marching orders to be Compleated to 36 rounds per man.[3]

This plate is a re-creation of the British infantry during that unsuccessful 1758 campaign. The rifleman carries a German jaeger-type weapon — probably sent over from England, possibly locally procured. The other private's musket has been shortened; he carries twenty-four rounds in his regular cartridge box, twelve in an improvised waist box.[4] The waistcoats have not been shortened (since all accounts speak only of "coats"). Expecting action in the near future, their heavy knapsacks have been left behind under guard. The Indian is one of the few Mohawk scouts who were bribed and cajoled into accompanying the expedition, but proved almost useless.

This expensive shortening of coats, in an effort to develop a handy field uniform, would be replaced in 1759 by the conversion of the coat to a jerkin, its sleeves being sewn onto the waistcoat. A year later, General Jeffery Amherst would reach the logical conclusion of directing that the troops "go in their waistcoats."

One lesson of this 1758 campaign was that improved weapons, equipment, and uniforms would not guarantee success in forest fighting. Useful as these might be, the major problem was that of acclimatizing British — and most American — troops to the somber North American wilderness, which affected them much as the jungles of the Southwest Pacific did American soldiers in World War II.

Frederick E. Ray, Jr.
John R. Elting

[1] Norreys J. O'Conor. *Servant of the Crown in England and in North America 1756-1761.* New York: Appleton-Century, 1938. pp. 92-95.
[2] Cecil C.P. Lawson. *A History of the Uniforms of the British Army.* Vol. III. London: Kaye & Ward, 1961. pp. 77-79.
[3] O'Conor. *Ibid.,* pp. 96-101 and John R. Cuneo. *Robert Rogers of the Rangers.* New York: Oxford Univ. Press. 1959. pp. 71, 82.
[4] Lawson. *Ibid.,* p. 47; and Harold L. Peterson. *Arms and Armor in Colonial America 1526-1783.* Harrisburg: Stackpole, 1956. pp. 235-237.

Private

Rifleman   Officer

55th Regiment of Foot, 1758

60th (Royal American) Regiment of Foot, 1755-1763

Braddock's disaster at the Monongahela in 1755 led the British government to authorize — after much backbiting and delay — the raising of a four-battalion regiment, to be recruited in Germany, and among the Swiss and German settlers in Pennsylvania and Maryland, for service in North America. This idea seems to have originated with one James (or Jacques) Prevost, an incompetent Swiss adventurer who apparently was fleeing from a French court-martial. By glibness and effrontery Prevost gained the support of the bumbling Duke of Cumberland, then Commander-in-Chief of the British Army. He was authorized to raise a number of Protestant Swiss and German officers and sergeants, who would sail for America to recruit the four battalions up to their approved strength of 1,000 each. Later 400 more Germans were recruited. The Earl of Loudoun, the new British commander in North America, was made Colonel-in-Chief but each battalion was to have a "colonel commandant." By good fortune the foreign officers included several outstanding soldiers, notably Henry Bouquet and Frederick Haldimand.

This regiment was designated the 62d (Royal American) Regiment of Foot. But neither Prevost nor Cumberland, nor the British officials involved with its conception, had the least knowledge of North America. Recruits were hard to find: Bouquet and Haldimand, respectively lieutenant colonels of the 1st and 2d battalions, were first on the ground and probably enlisted most of the Americans available. Even so, Bouquet had only 547 men by December 1756. In February 1757, following the "breaking" of the 50th and 51st regiments, most of which had been captured at Oswego by the French, the Royal Americans were renumbered the 60th Regiment. Probably no odder unit ever carried the proud designation "Royal."[1] During 1756-1763 its personnel were roughly one-fourth assorted Americans, over one-half unwanted yardbirds drafted out of the British regiments in Ireland, and the rest miscellaneous Germans, Poles, and Bohemians. The 60th still was recruiting in Germany in 1767. It included volunteers — allegedly "Germans" — from among French prisoners of war, and sergeants, corporals, invalids, and apprehended deserters from the 50th and 51st.[2]

The battalions varied greatly. Skilled in European partisan warfare and quick to adapt it to American conditions, Bouquet made his 1st Battalion into light infantry specially trained for forest warfare. The 2nd and 3rd battalions were little different from average British infantry. Prevost's 4th Battalion was a military madhouse. Prevost himself was universally despised for his ignorance, insolence, and brutality, but could not be disciplined because he was Cumberland's protege.

The 60th served in all the important campaigns from 1757 on. Its 2nd and 3rd Battalions were at the surrender of Louisbourg and Quebec; the 1st at the capture of Fort Duquesne and in the Carolinas. During 1763, scattered garrisons of the Royal Americans met the first shock of Pontiac's Rebellion; in 1764 they had a share in its final quelling. Seven years of wilderness campaigning had left the whole regiment half-mutinous, with many desertions. Captain Simon Ecuyer described his garrison at Fort Pitt as ". . . a gang of mutineers, bandits, cut-throats, especially the grenadiers . . ." but he held the Fort with them nevertheless.[3] The regiment remained in America until 1775, when it was transferred to the West Indies.

Being a "royal" regiment, the 60th had blue facings. Unlike other British regiments, however, the enlisted men's uniforms were without lace until sometime after 1763.[4] There is no known contemporary picture of the Royal Americans for 1755-1760; and details of their uniform such as the grenadier caps, must be reconstructed from the Royal Warrant of 1751. Deserter descriptions in New York and Philadelphia newspapers frequently mention leather breeches, as worn by the private in the right foreground of this plate, and red waistcoats; this combination may have been a summer service uniform. Brown canvas "marching gaiters" were common wear, white gaiters being reserved for full dress. Officers wore silver lace.[5] The plate illustrates how the uniform coat could be worn either with its lapels buttoned back, or closed across the chest. To make them less conspicuous, the belts were not pipeclayed white. After a few months' campaigning, the sergeant probably would exchange his halberd for a musket.

Bouquet, at least, adopted articles of frontier dress for his battalion. In 1758, it apparently wore hunting shirts and Indian leggings.[6] The next year a letter from one of his subordinates states ". . . our people have leggings. I intended always they should have been blue, but we could not have blue at Albany, so that we have green tied with a red garter."[7]

Originally the 60th was issued ". . . 3741 long land service Musquets of the King's Pattern . . . deemed serviceable but not fit for regular regiments."[8] Because the 60th later became the famous Royal Rifle Corps, many myths have developed around its service in America, for example, that it wore green uniforms and was armed with rifles. In fact, it remained basically a red-coated infantry regiment until after 1813.

Frederick E. Ray, Jr.
Frederick P. Todd
John R. Elting

[1]Stanley McC. Pargellis. *Lord Loudoun in North America* New Haven: Yale University Press, 1933. pp. 61-67. Loudoun's commission, dated December 24, 1755, is considered the Regiment's birthday, but final approval came only on March 9, 1756.

[2]*Ibid.* pp. 111-112. The 50th and 51st Foot were mostly Americans.

[3]Francis Parkman. *The Conspiracy of Pontiac.* New York: Collier Books, 1962. p. 379.

[4]René Chartrand "Uniforms of the British Army in North America, 1761." *Military Collector & Historian.* Vol. 24, Summer, 1972. p. 58.

[5]Cecil C.P. Lawson. *A History of the Uniforms of the British Army,* Vol. III, London: Kaye & Ward, 1961. pp. 210-212, includes a purported portrait of Bouquet.

[6]Douglas S. Freeman: *George Washington,* Vol. II, New York: Charles Scribner, 1948. p. 316.

[7]Lawson, *Ibid.* p. 212.   [8]Pargellis, *Ibid.* p. 66.

Private, Bn. Co.   Officer, Grenadier Co.   Private, Bn. Co.   Sergeant, Bn. Co.

60th (Royal American) Regiment of Foot, 1755-1763

78th (Highland) Regiment of Foot, (Fraser's Highlanders), 1757-1763

This short-lived but famous regiment was raised at Inverness, Scotland in 1757 as the "2nd Highland Battalion of Foot," specifically for service in North America. Its organizer and commander was Simon Fraser, Master of Lovat, who had fought for Bonnie Prince Charlie in 1745. Officers and men were Frasers, Campbells, MacPhersons, MacDonalds, Camerons, Stewarts, Cuthberts, Baillies, Menzies, and MacAllisters. Their speech among themselves was Gaelic, and they were either Presbyterian or Catholic. Both sects went respectfully before their Presbyterian chaplain, big, horse-strong Reverend Robert McPherson.

Recruited to full strength — 59 officers including chaplain, adjutant, quartermaster, and surgeon; 40 sergeants; 40 corporals; 20 drummers; and 1,000 "private men" — the 78th embarked at Glasgow in April 1757 accompanied by 170 additional volunteers and an unspecified number of regimental women. The presence of the supernumerary volunteers led the British government to authorize all Highland units three additional companies in July 1757; another company was added in 1758. Fraser's "battalion" therefore came to have fourteen companies, with a total strength of 1,542 officers and men — half again as strong as the average British regiment.

The 78th spent the winter of 1757-1758 in Connecticut where it found good quarters — and also good New England rum, which proved mightier than usquebaugh. After its first encounter with this beverage the 78th reportedly was drunk for three days, to the distress of proper General Jeffery Amherst. But discipline, the Reverend MacPherson, and training by American rangers in forest warfare brought the 78th through the winter in excellent condition. The next spring it was back at Halifax where sour-minded General James Wolfe conceded that the Highlanders were "... very useful serviceable soldiers, and commanded by the most manly corps of officers. ..."[1]

The 78th played a creditable part in the capture of Louisbourg that summer and in the capture and subsequent defense of Quebec in 1759-1760. Detachments took part in the capture of Montreal in 1760 and the recovery of St. John's, Newfoundland in 1761. The 78th was disbanded at Quebec in December 1763, grants of land being awarded those who were willing to remain in Canada.

The uniform of the 78th is succinctly described in *A List of His Majesty's Land Forces in North America, with the Rank of the Officers in the Regiment and Army, 1761* (New York, 1861) — "Seventy Eight Regiment . . . Lieutenant Colonel Commander Simon Fraser . . . Uniform, Red faced White, Belted Plaid and Hose."[2] It is certain that officers and sergeants had scarlet coats, laced respectively with gold and silver; "other ranks" had the usual brick red with white lace. Hose were the familiar red and white chequer, gartered with scarlet tape. The coats, at least until 1760, seem to have been without lapels.[3] The blue bonnets had a plain red band and a red tuft, and were worn "with a slight band enclining down to the right ear,

over which were suspended two or more black feathers."[4] Sporrans were of plain leather or badger or other skins, provided by the men according to their individual whim. Enlisted men's buttons and buckles were white metal, except for the shoe buckles which apparently were brass. Officers' buttons may have been gold, but the rest of their metal was silver.

Insofar as can be determined, Fraser's Highlanders wore the "Government Tartan," similar to that of the 42nd Foot. Its colors were lighter and softer than in the modern version, and there was considerable variation in shades and pattern, since the cloth was made up by many weavers. The 78th may have added an overstripe of some other color, as was done in the 42nd for its grenadier company, but this is only a possibility.[5]

For weapons, the government issued firelocks, bayonets, "side pistols," and broadswords, with halberds for the sergeants. The type of musket issued remains an interesting question: several companies left at Louisbourg in 1759 had to exchange theirs for the "heavy arms" of the soldiers detailed to the expedition's provisional light infantry unit.[6] This suggests that at least part of the 78th had the shorter, light muskets of the artillery or "sea-service" types. Enlisted men's broadswords had black-lacquered hilts.

The 78th was raised for active service at the end of a difficult supply line. Although by 1762-1763 it might have become somewhat more elaborately uniformed, during the winter of 1759-1760 one of its officers wryly noted that ". . . the Philabeg [little kilt] is not all calculated for this terrible climate. Colonel Fraser is doing all in his power to provide trousers . . ."[7]

In this plate, the officer is in campaign dress, with only a touch of gold lace on his waistcoat. In the field, he probably would have carried a fusee. By contrast, the sergeant is in full glory of scarlet, silver lace, and belted plaid — possibly with future "fraternization" in mind. The piper has the uniform of his fellow soldiers as seems to have been common in all Highland regiments at this time. All of them show typical effects of North American service: strips of bearskin have replaced their black cockades; the sergeant has a musket instead of a halberd; and sashes, aiguillettes, and such trimmings have vanished.

Frederick T. Chapman
John R. Elting

[1]James Roy. *Lieutenant-General Simon Fraser.* An unpublished biography of Simon Fraser, p. 43.

[2]René Chartrand. "Uniforms of the British Army in North America, 1761," *Military Collector & Historian,* Vol. 24, Summer 1972. p. 58 and Roy. *Ibid.* p. 36.

[3]Officers may have lapelled coats for dress. See 42d Regiment of Foot, page 2, this volume.

[4]David Stewart. *Sketches of the Character, Manners and Present State of the Highlanders of Scotland,* II. Edinburgh, 1822, p. 12.

[5]Roy. *Ibid.* p. 36. A thorough check by the Court of the Lord Lyon and The Scottish Tartan Society failed to produce evidence of any "Fraser" or "Lovat" tartan. The so-called "Red Fraser" is comparatively modern.

[6]Captain John Knox, as quoted in Cecil C. P. Lawson. *A History of the Uniforms of the British Army.* Vol. II. London: Kaye & Ward, 1961. p. 46.   [7]Roy. *Ibid.* p. 69.   [8]Stewart. *Ibid.* p. 68.

78th (Highland) Regiment of Foot (Fraser's Highlanders), 1757-1763

Gorham's Rangers, 1759-1761

Gorham's Rangers began as Captain John Gorham's "Indian Rangers of the Woods," described as mostly full-blooded, practically naked Mohawk warriors with a sprinkling of half-clad half-breeds sent by Governor William Shirley to relieve Annapolis Royal, Nova Scotia in 1744.[1] In 1747, George II was ". . . pleased to grant a commission to Captain Gorham to command a Company of One Hundred men to be employed for the defense of His Majesty's fortress of Annapolis and Province of Nova Scotia . . . It is apprehended that the case of this gentleman is so particular and the service he has and may render great, that no inconvenience can arise from this mark of favor to him."[2] Gorham's Rangers carried the brunt of the defense of Nova Scotia throughout 1747-1749, supported by two armed sloops owned by Gorham. Operating by water or cross country, he cowed the Indian tribes and Acadians and rapidly extended the area of English authority. In 1749, Gorham's Company was put on the Nova Scotia Establishment, thus becoming a regular unit. Although the War of the Austrian Succession, or King George's War, supposedly had ended in 1748, fighting went on savagely in Nova Scotia until 1751.

Recruiting continued during this period. In October 1750, for example, an advertisement in the *Boston Weekly News* challenged "gentlemen volunteers" and others to apply for service in the Independent Companies of Rangers in Nova Scotia. Applicants were promised entertainment at the Sign of the Lamb, a tavern in the south end of Boston, as well as "present pay" and uniforms of blue broadcloth. There was also a discreet mention of bounty money for Indian scalps.

John Gorham died in 1751, and was succeeded by his brother, First Lieutenant Joseph Gorham. In 1759 the Company was one of the six Ranger companies used by Major General James Wolfe in his attack on Quebec. Usually referred to as "Major", Joseph Gorham seems to have been the senior Ranger officer present and certainly served as a task force commander, screening the flanks and rear of Wolfe's army throughout the campaign. In 1761, he was rewarded with a major's commission in the British Army. From 1761-1764, Gorham commanded the "Corps of Rangers" or "North American Rangers" which apparently consisted of his own and one or more additional companies. These units were disbanded between 1763-1764 after elements had served against Pontiac.

The first description of the uniform of Gorham's Rangers after the 1750 Boston advertisement appears in the Loudoun papers where an entry for January 15-30, 1757, states, "The Irregulars in Nova Scotia are Payed on the Regular Troops are cloathed by the Board of Trade and have Leather Caps. They have powder horns in place of Cartridge Boxes." Recruiting advertisements for that year offer merely a "new good full suit of Cloaths" with no mention of uniforms. Captain John Knox, in Nova Scotia, noted that the rangers wore ordinary clothing "cut short."

In May 1759, however, Knox entered in his journal:

The rangers have got a new uniform clothing; the ground is of black ratteen or frize, lapelled and cuffed with blue; here follows a description of their dress; a waistcoat with sleeves; a short jacket without sleeves; only armholes and wings to the shoulders (in like manner as the Grenadiers and Drummers of the army) white metal buttons, linen or canvas drawers, with a blue skirt or petticoat of stuff, made with a waistband and one button; this open before and does not quite extend to their knees; a pair of leggins of the same color with their coat, which reach up to the middle of the thighs (without flaps) and from the calf of the leg downward they button like spatterdashes; with this active dress they wear blue bonnets, and I think, in great measure resemble our Highlanders.[3]

This uniform was undoubtedly worn by all six of the Ranger companies with Wolfe. The skirt must have been for warmth on boat expeditions or while waiting in ambush. It could be quickly detached for movement through brush. The leggings, which all of the figures in this plate wear, were a modification of Indian gear. Made of doubled layers of woolen cloth, these gave the legs both more freedom of action and better protection than the regulation spatterdashes. English regiments frequently adopted them for wear in the field. Green boughs in the hats were a common English recognition signal.

Two years later, in 1761, five members of Major Gorham's Company of Rangers deserted from Fort Frederick. "The above Persons," said the deserter description printed in the *Boston News-Letter*, "were clothed in the Uniform of the Company, viz. Coats, red turn'd up with brown, with brown Capes and brown Insides, which may be worn either Side out; Waistcoats of the brown Colour; Linnen Draws; leather Jockey-Caps, with Oak-Leaf or Branch painted on the left Side . . ." This uniform, as shown in this plate, would be adaptable to either field or garrison duty. The equipment shown follows light infantry practice, itself adapted from ranger usage. The survival of the leather caps mentioned by Loudoun earlier is interesting.

Another possible uniform is mentioned in the newspaper description of a sergeant deserter in 1763: "Had on when he went away a red Coat, Waistcoat, and Breeches, with Silver Vellum Button Holes to the Coat and Waistcoat." This sounds as if the Rangers had been getting very regulation about their dress, though privates deserting during the same period wore nondescript civilian clothing.

Frederick Ray
John R. Elting

[1]*Collections of the Nova Scotia Historical Society*, Vol. 30, 1954. pp. 28-29. The spelling "Goreham" is often encountered, but "Gorham" is correct.
[2]*Ibid.* p. 44.
[3]John Knox. *A Historical Journal of the Campaigns in North America for the Years, 1757, 1758, 1759 and 1760.* Toronto: The Champlain Society, 1914. Vol. I, p. 307; and Stanley McC. Pargellis. *Military Affairs in North America, 1748-1760.* New York: D. Appleton, 1936.

Ranger, 1759   Officer, 1761   Rangers, 1761

Gorham's Rangers, 1759-1761

The Charleston Artillery Company, 1756-1768

In the fall of 1756, about 60 gentlemen in the Charleston Regiment of Militia organized themselves into a company of artillery, which was to be clothed in a proper uniform, exercised with firelocks as well as with cannon, and commanded by an officer experienced in gunnery.[1] A petition for the establishment of the company was sent to the governor in January 1757 and was approved by both the governor and the Commons House.[2]

The uniform is described as blue broadcloth coatees, lapelled, lined, and cuffed with crimson cloth; gilt buttons; crimson jackets; blue breeches, white stockings, and gold laced hats. The officers wore the same, except that their lapels and cuffs were of crimson velvet. A waist and a shoulder belt of dressed leather, a black cartouche box, a firelock, and a bayonet were the equipment of the private men. Officers were armed with a fusee, a cartouche box, and a sword.[3]

In November 1759, when Governor Lyttelton and 1500 militia set out to impose a new treaty on the Cherokee Nation, twenty volunteers from the Artillery Company, commanded by their captain, accompanied the expedition. They were wearing their uniforms, were completely armed and accoutered, and were all on horseback, escorting two small brass field pieces and their ammunition carts. Their drivers seem to have been negroes. The 500-mile campaign which ended in mid-January made real field artillerymen out of them.[4] A detachment of the Royal Regiment of Artillery arrived in Charleston in December 1759, having been sent by General Amherst for the express purpose of training the Charleston Artillery Company. They departed the end of April 1760 with everyone well pleased with the results.[5]

In June 1760 the alarm was "fired," and half of the militia, including half of the Artillery Company, was drafted to march against the Creek Indians. It was soon determined that a series of unrelated incidents had been mistaken for the early stages of a war with the whole Creek Nation, and the militia was disbanded.[6] In July 1760, a militia act dealing only with the Artillery Company was passed, putting the already-established company on a legal basis and spelling out its organization: one captain, one captain-lieutenant, one first and one second lieutenant, three lieutenant fireworkers, four sergeants, and not more than 100 private men (to be classed as bombardiers, gunners, and matrosses). Every person in the compay was to be approved by the captain and was to provide himself with the required clothes, arms, ammunition, and accoutrements, after which he was exempt from service in the militia. When the unit was ordered into service in case of alarm, the public was to furnish an artillery chest, powder carts, and ammunition wagons.[7]

During the Cherokee War, a small train of artillery accompanied the South Carolina Provincial Regiment in Lieutenant Colonel Grant's expedition of 1761.[8] It consisted of two field pieces and four cohorns mounted on field carriages, with a plentiful quantity of fixed ammunition and laboratory stores, under the command of an officer of the Artillery Company. However, the artillery probably did not go beyond Fort Prince George (250 miles from Charleston) because the mountain trails thereafter limited transportation to pack horses.

On the King's Birthday in 1768, the Artillery Company was paraded in "a new and very genteel uniform": blue coatees, lined, lapelled, and cuffed with crimson; gilt buttons; white waistcoats, breeches, and stockings; and gold laced hats. There is some evidence that the old breeches and waistcoats were still worn during cold weather up until 1775. The officers wore gold aguillettes to indicate their rank. That same year the Commons House authorized the payment of 700 pounds to the captain of the Company for the purchase of two brass three-pounder field pieces with proper shot.[9]

Peter F. Copeland
Fitzhugh McMaster

[1] South Carolina Gazette; September 2, October 21, and December 9, 1756 (Library Society, Charleston, S. C.); Sainsbury Facsimilies of BPRO, Vol. XXVII, p. 347 (S. C. Archives).

[2] Commons House Journal, November 1756-July 1757, Part II, pp. 21, 23, 25, 30, 42-43 (MS, S. C. Archives); South Carolina Gazette, January 20, 1757.

[3] South Carolina Gazette. Ibid. August 18, 1757, November 17, 1758 and Supplement; and Thomas Cooper Statutes at Large of South Carolina, Columbia, S. C., 1841, Vol. IX, p. 640.

[4] South Carolina Gazette. October 12, November 1, 1759, January 12, 1760.

[5] Ibid. December 8, 1759, February 2, April 26, and May 3, 1760.

[6] Ibid. June 7, 1760, and Council Journal, April-December 1760, pp. 131-133 in South Carolina Archives.

[7] Thomas Cooper. Ibid. Vol. IX, pp. 664-666.

[8] Commons House Journal, October 1760-January 1761, part II, pp. 22-23, S. C. Archives; South Carolina Gazette, December 6, 1760.

[9] South Carolina Gazette: June 6, 1768; Charleston Year Book, 1889, Appendix (Diary of Bernard Elliott, Charleston, S.C., 1889); Commons House Journal, November 1767-November 1768, p. 638, S.C. Archives.

PC₇₂

Driver

Matross, 1759

Officer, 1768

Officer, 1759

The Charleston Artillery Company, 1756-1768

The New Jersey Regiment (Jersey Blues), 1755-1764

Early in 1755 the provincial government of New Jersey authorized the raising of five companies for service against the French.[1] By May their organization was complete, and they were combined into a regiment. Shortly thereafter, they were ordered to the northern frontier under command of Colonel Peter Schuyler, a provincial officer who had commanded the troops from New Jersey during the campaigns of 1746-1748. These earlier men had been called "Jersey Blues" and, since the new Regiment also wore a blue uniform, the name was applied to them as well.

Apparently the Regiment returned to New Jersey for the winter 1755-1756. In the spring of 1756, it returned north where half of it was stationed at Schenectady and the other half at Oswego. This latter part was captured, along with Schuyler himself, by Montcalm's army on August 14. The command then went to Captain John Parker and ill-luck continued. On July 21, 1757, the Regiment lost heavily in the affair at Sabbath Day Point, and the following month all the men and officers who remained (301) were captured at the fall of Fort William Henry and paroled for eighteen months.

In the spring of 1758, the Regiment was "augmented," or really re-raised, under command of Colonel John Johnson, and took part in the disastrous campaign of that year against Fort Ticonderoga. At this time the unit consisted of almost 1000 men. In 1759, it was again recruited up to this number and commanded once more by Peter Schuyler, who had been released. It served until November.

It was raised again by the act of March 25, 1760 to 1000 men and employed chiefly at Oswego. This year, apparently, it had an attached company of rangers. In 1761, it was raised to a strength of 600 men and officers and served until November. One company continued in service through the winter, and the following spring the Regiment was recruited up to 665 men and officers. It is not clear if the command served in 1763, but the next year the Regiment was raised once more to 600 men and served that summer at Oswego. Apparently it was then finally disbanded.

For some reason which is not obvious, the New Jersey Regiment was a superior unit in all ways. It enjoyed a splendid reputation for discipline, character of personnel, dress, and general reliability. After the Regiment passed through New York in June 1758, a newspaper called them "the likeliest well-set Men for the Purpose as has perhaps been turned out on any Campaign ... their uniform blue, faced with red, grey stockings and Buckskin Breeches."[2] Governor Barnard of New Jersey wrote William Pitt in March of the next year that "these men are sent into the field in a different manner from those of most other provinces: they are completely cloathed in a handsome uniform & furnished with all necessaries: and they are muster'd to a Man: in both which articles several of the other provinces are greatly deficient."[3]

Only one painting exists — that of Colonel Schuyler himself now in the New Jersey Historical Society, at Newark. The Act of the New Jersey Assembly which authorized the regiment in 1758, however, contains a fine statement of its accoutrements. It provided for a "blue Coat, after the Highland Manner, Lappell'd and cuffed with red, one pair of Ticken Breeches, one Blue ditto of the same cloath of their Coat, one Check Shirt, and one white ditto, two pair yarn Stockings, two pair of Shoes, one Hat to each Man, bound with yellow Binding, one Blanket, one Knapsack, one Hatchet, one Canteen, one Camp Kettle to five Men, a pair of White Patterdashes and also one hundred Grenadiers Caps for one hundred of the said soldiers and two felling axes for the whole Regiment."

H. Charles McBarron, Jr.
Frederick P. Todd

[1] This historical account is based upon documents in *New Jersey Archives*. 1st series, Vols. VIII-X, *passim; New York Colonial Documents*, Vol. X, pp. 443-4, 591-2, 617, 624, 732; and local New Jersey histories.

[2] *New York Mercury*, June 5, 1758.

[3] *New Jersey Archives*, 1st series, Vol. VIII, part 2, p. 167. "Mustered to a man" meant "at full authorized strength."

Company Officer and Grenadier, parade order   *Private, marching order*   *Light Infantryman*

The New Jersey Regiment (Jersey Blues), 1755-1764

Captain Hezekiah Dunn's Company of Rangers, New Jersey Frontier Guard, 1756-1760

On January 9, 1758, the *New York Gazette* carried an advertisement for a deserter from "Captain Hezekiah Dunn's Company of Rangers" . . . "Provincial clothing viz. A grey lapell'd Waistcoat and an under green Jacket, a Leather Cap, and Buckskin Breeches." Obviously, both the captain and his unit were well-known by their contemporaries, but his name did not appear on the surviving muster rolls of any known ranger company.

Two hundred and three years later, considerable — and long-frustrated — research finally nailed down the mysterious Hezekiah.

In the fall of 1756 the Province of New Jersey organized a company of rangers, usually referred to as "The Frontier Guard," to protect its western boundaries during the winter from the constant and costly Indian raids. A second company was raised in September 1757, to consist of "One Hundred Men, Officers included": a captain, two lieutenants, four sergeants, four corporals, and 89 private men. This seems to have been Dunn's company;[1] the earlier company apparently had been commanded by a Captain Gardiner, who was later recommended by the Governor for promotion to major.

Records so far uncovered are vague. Two companies seem to have been in service under Gardiner during the summer of 1758. A British letter of December 12, 1757 mentions "Captain Dunn of the New Jersey Ranging Company." To support them, the governor had ordered four colonels of militia to hold a detail of fifty men ready from each of their regiments.[2] In July 1760, there is a hazy reference to a company of 120 New Jersey rangers under Captain Gardiner at Oswego, New York.[3]

The Frontier Guard's original uniform is definitely stated in the *Votes and Proceedings of the General Assembly of the Province of New Jersey, August 19-23 September 1757*. . . . "And each Officer and Soldier furnished at the Expence of this Colony, with a good Blanket, a Half-thick Under-Jacket, a Kersey Jacket Lapell'd, Buckskin Breeches, two Pair of Shoes, and two pair of Stockings, and a Leather Cap, and a Hatchet." The pay was ranger pay, the captain drawing six shillings a day, and each private three. Being rangers, they would be expected to furnish their own weapons; these undoubtedly included a high proportion of rifles. Note that these are "provincial rangers," raised and paid by New Jersey, and not — like Gorham's and Roger's rangers — by the British Government.

In a successful skirmish against a party of fifty Indians, which had "murdered the seven New-York Soldiers at Westfalls" on June 13, 1758, the rangers are described as laying aside their "Packs and Hats" before crawling up on the enemy encampment, and thereafter as fighting from tree to tree.[4] Hats would certainly be more comfortable than the leather caps during a New Jersey summer. At the same time, the under jacket alone would suffice for summer service.

The ranger on the left, dressed for summer, totes an Indian-style pack, suspended across his chest and shoulders by a "tumpline." His musket, cartridge box, and bayonet are probably from the 2000 stand of arms purchased by New Jersey in 1757. The other three rangers carry rifles and have suited their own fancies and conveniences in the way of field equipment. The officer has added a short cutting sword as a badge of rank, and wears his bullet pouch on the front of his waist belt, after the fashion of Rogers' Rangers. The man in the right foreground, like many a seasoned campaigner in other wars, has rolled up his possessions within his blanket; his bullet pouch is made of an otter skin, and his leggings of blue blanket cloth, with its selvedge left on as ornamental trim.

H. Charles McBarron, Jr.
John R. Elting

[1] *New Jersey Archives*, First Series, Vol. XVII.
[2] Letter, Governor Bernard to the Lords Commissioners of Trades and Plantations, July 3, 1758.
[3] T. F. Gordon, *History of New Jersey*, Philadelphia: 1834.
[4] *The Pennsylvania Journal*, No. 813, July 6, 1758.

Summer Dress   *Officer*

Captain Hezekiah Dunn's Company of Rangers, New Jersey Frontier Guard, 1756-1760

The Pennsylvania Regiment, 1756-1758

The Regiment was born out of the Pennsylvania border massacres perpetrated in 1755 by the Susquehanna and Ohio Delawares. A militia bill passed November 25, 1755 mobilized the frontiersmen.[1] The first companies were merely old volunteer units taken into regular service, or raised by men holding the Governor's commission. In March 1756 the companies east of the Susquehanna were formed into a battalion under Lieutenant Colonel Conrad Weiser; those west of the river under Lieutenant Colonel John Armstrong. Colonel William Clapham raised a third battalion to erect and garrison Fort Augusta and its environs. Later these forces were formed into two regiments: Clapham's became the 1st (Augusta) Regiment, while the other two comprised the 2nd (Pennsylvania) Regiment. By 1758 Weiser's battalion was broken up and its companies assigned to the other two units. These were again regimented under Governor William Denny, with Armstrong commanding the 1st Battalion and Lieutenant Colonel James Burd the 2nd.

Twenty-three companies of "new levies" were raised for 1758; sixteen formed a 3rd Battalion under Hugh Mercer, while seven were assigned to Armstrong and Burd. These levies were discharged at the end of the campaign.[2]

None of the troops were uniformed at first, but by February 1757 it was decided the men should wear green coats, red jackets and buckskin breeches. As to the civilian garb then in use, we have this query regarding the new levies of 1758:

> Must the men buy green Cloathing? I fear this will hurt us much. I think linnen Stockings, red below the Knee, Petticoat Trousers, reaching to the thick of the Leg, made of Strong Linnen, and a Sailor's Frock made of the same, would be best. Young men that have Cloathing (especially Dutch) will not like to lay out their Money for more.[3]

Some men wore blue stockings, light colored coats and white linen or cotton caps.[4]

In 1758 General John Forbes ordered that all the new levies be uniformed in "short green coats, lapell'd with the same."[5] This might suggest that Weiser's old battalion had green facings, while deserter reports indicate red facings for Armstrong's and the old Augusta Regiment. With the reorganization of 1757-58, doubtless some companies had green facings and some red in both battalions, but as early as June 1757 one deserter was wearing a "blue coat, faced with red." Blue regi-mentals are more often mentioned in the 1759-61 period.[6]

Colonel Henry Bouquet of the Royal Americans suggested to Forbes that some provincials be dressed in the Indian manner: ". . . remove their coats and breeches, which will delight them, give them moccasins and blankets; cut off their hair and daub them with paint." When Colonel George Washington's Virginians showed up at Raystown in this garb, Bouquet assured him that "Their dress should be our pattern in this expedition." Later he added, "It takes very well here, and thank God, we See nothing but Shirts and Blanketts, & a."[7]

The arms furnished by the Province were poor. They were heavy, rusty and apt to burst; stocks were cracked and broken, and the screw plates often tied on with string. Recruits were encouraged to bring their own guns, and many brought rifles.[8] The government supplied cartridge boxes and tomahawks, although Bouquet noted a lack of the latter in 1758, as well as any kind of camp gear. That year a company in each of the 1st and 2nd Battalions was replaced by a troop of light horse, but Bouquet didn't admire them either: "The sabers, or rather hangers, which were given to the light cavalry are a joke. It is their principal weapon and they could not kill a chicken with this tiny knife."[9]

In this plate, the two enlisted men have Indian leggings, the left-hand figure's being the military version. The center figure wears a hunting shirt. Both men in uniform wear buckskin breeches — a durable and cheap article of clothing.

Eric I. Manders

[1] William A. Hunter. *Forts on the Pennsylvania Frontier 1753-1758.* Harrisburg: Pennsylvania Historical and Museum Commission, 1960. pp. 184-186.

[2] *Ibid.* pp. 202-206.

[3] *Ibid.* p. 199.

[4] Descriptions of deserters from the Pennsylvania Regiment, 1757-61, furnished by John R. Elting.

[5] Hunter. *Ibid.* p. 199. Stevenson to Bouquet, June 2, 1758.

[6] Most of these had red facings, but one at least had "blue Facings, and yellow worked Button Holes."

[7] Hunter. *Ibid.* pp. 199-200.

[8] A soldier was allowed a half dollar each for the use of his own blanket and gun. Commonwealth of Pennsylvania. *Report of the Commission to Locate the Site of the Frontier Forts of Pennsylvania.* Harrisburg: 1896. Vol. I, pp. 11, 301.

[9] Charles Morse Stotz. *Defense in the Wilderness.* Published in the Historical Society of Western Pennsylvania. *Drums in the Forest.* Pittsburgh: 1958. pp. 103-104.

The Pennsylvania Regiment, 1756-1758

The Virginia Regiment, 1754-1762

Early in 1754, the Colony of Virginia, under pressure from the French in the Ohio Valley, raised two volunteer companies from the militia for service on the frontier. At the same time, Lieutenant Governor Robert Dinwiddie sought to enlist a regiment of six companies, all volunteers. George Washington was appointed lieutenant colonel, and Joshua Fry, colonel. This was the start of the Virginia Regiment and at least five companies were recruited by mid-year.[1]

In October 1754, the Regiment was broken up into ten independent companies with no field officers, but it was incorporated again in 1755 with sixteen companies. Washington was appointed colonel; Adam Stephen, lieutenant colonel; and Andrew Lewis, major. Washington formally assumed command on September 17, 1755.[2]

Details of the uniform of the Virginia Regiment are numerous but conflicting. At its start, the men were expected to wear their civilian clothing but Washington quickly saw the fallacy of this plan and wrote Dinwiddie from Alexandria on March 9, 1754:

> We daily experience the great necessity for cloathing the men, as we find the generality of those, who are to be enlisted, are of those loose, idle persons that are quite destitute of House and Home, and, I may truly say, many of them of Cloaths . . . there is many of them without Shoes, others want Stockings, some are without Shirts, and not a few have scarce a Coat or Waistcoat to their backs . . . I really believe every man of them, for their own credits sake, is willing to be Cloathed at their own expense.[3]

The Governor raised no objection to uniforms provided care "be taken of buying the cloth at the cheapest rate," and he authorized Washington to deduct enough from the men's pay "to purchase a Coat and Breeches of red Cloth."[4]

This first uniform is suggested by a description of several deserters dated April 12, 1754 at Alexandria. Two men wore "Thunder and Lightning Jackets; one had red, and the other Leather Breeches. They took their Arms with them, having Virginia, 1750, engraved on the Barrels." One deserter had "a red Coat turn'd up with blue," but three others wore simply "red Coats." All three had leather breeches.[5]

Exactly what was meant by a "Thunder and Lightning Jacket" is not clear, but it is safe to assume that the uniform coat provided was the simplest style then in use, without lapels, buttoned across the front — the type worn by the Regiment of Invalids and some other corps. It would have been easy for local workers to fashion belts and cartridge boxes based upon British army patterns. Linen haversacks were made by the companies themselves; each man provided his own blanket. Muskets were taken from State militia stores.

Apparently, officers wore scarlet coats. There is a reference to Major Adam Stephen donning a "flaming suit of laced regimentals" during the affair at Fort Necessity in 1755.[6] When the Regiment was reorganized, the uniform was changed to blue, faced with red, as indicated by a general order published at Fort Cumberland on September 17, 1755:

> Every officer of the Virginia Regiment to provide himself as soon as he can conveniently with a suit of Regimentals of good blue Cloath; the Coat to be faced and cuffed with Scarlet, and trimmed with silver; a Scarlet wasitcoat, with Silver Lace; blue Breeches, and a Silver-laced Hat, if to be had, for Camp and Garrison Duty. Besides this, each Officer is to provide himself with a common soldiers Dress, for Detachments and Duty in the Woods.[7]

This apparently remained the uniform of the officers throughout the period of the war. It is the uniform worn by Washington in the portrait by Charles Willson Peale, painted in 1772, except that the breeches in the portrait are scarlet.

The enlisted mens' uniform was changed at the same time. It is fairly certain that some of the Virginia companies with Braddock in the summer of 1775 had bob-tailed their coats and it seems likely that they remained bobbed as shown in the plate. Apparently, there was a fairly regular issue of clothing, although Washington several times had to complain to Dinwiddie about its poor quality and frequent shortages.

In 1758, a 2nd Virginia Regiment was raised under command of Colonel William Byrd, but it was mustered out in December of the same year. Finally, in 1762, at Fort Lewis, Virginia the old Regiment came to an end.[8]

Frederick T. Chapman
Tom Parker

[1]Douglas S. Freeman. *George Washington: A Biography*. New York: Scribner, 1948. Vol. I, pp. 328-411.

[2]*Ibid.* pp. 412; J. C. Fitzpatrick. *Writings of Washington*. Bicentennial Edition. Washington: U.S.G.P.O. 1931. Vol. I, pp. 102, 160, Note 175.

[3]Fitzpatrick. *Ibid.* Vol. I, p. 32.

[4]R. A. Brock, ed. *The Official Records of Robert Dinwiddie, Lieutenant Governor of the Colony of Virginia, 1751-1758*. Richmond: Virginia Historical Society, 1883-84. Vol. I, letters of 15, 21 and 28 March pp. 106, 116, 120; F. R. Bellamy. *The Private Life of George Washington*. New York: Crowell, 1951. p. 74.

[5]*Maryland Gazette*, April 18, 1754.

[6]MS *"Life of Adam Stephen,"* in the Benjamin Rush Papers, Library Company of Philadelphia.

[7]Fitzpatrick, *Ibid.* Vol. I, p. 176-177. The order was repeated on October 5; *Ibid.* Vol. I, 185.

[8]Department of the Army, *Army Lineage Book, Infantry*, Vol. II, p. 504.

Field Officer and Private, 1754-1755   *Private and Company Officer, 1755-1762*

The Virginia Regiment, 1754-1762

French Colonial Infantry and Artillery, 1740-1763

Because they were administered by the Ministry of the Navy, the French colonies in America were garrisoned from the end of the 17th century by Independent Companies of the Navy (*Compagnies Franches de la Marine.*)[1] The men of these companies stood guard over the vast French territories extending from Guyana to Canada.

The duties of these colonial troops were as varied as the territories they guarded. In the outposts of Canada and Louisiana, they were Indian-style fighters. In Guyana and Saint Dominique, they pursued rebellious negroes in tropical forests. Most, however, were posted in large fortified towns like Quebec, Louisbourg, Cap Francais, and Fort Royal. The actions in which these troops took part were innumberable. They include both sieges of Louisbourg, the campaigns in Canada, the defense of Guadeloupe, Martinique, and the Ohio Valley. It should be noted that these colonial companies, with detachments of the Karrer Swiss Regiment, were the only regular troops in the French colonies until 1755. The survivors of the companies from Canada and Louisbourg were incorporated into Army battalions in 1760, those of Saint Dominique meeting the same fate in 1762, and those of Louisiana in 1763, when they were transferred to Saint Dominique, except for six companies which remained until a Spanish garrison arrived in 1769.[2] What remained of the *Cannoniers-Bombardiers* was incorporated into the two intact companies of Saint Dominique in 1762. These two companies were incorporated into the Army artillery in 1766.[3]

Although they bore the name "marine" (i.e. "navy"), these troops were in fact colonial regulars who had nothing to do with ships. The procurement of their officers directly from the colonies was encouraged and, for this purpose, the *Cadets a l'Equillette* were instituted during the 1730's.[4] Enlisted men generally came from France since it was hoped that they would settle in the colonies when their tours of duty had been completed.

The uniforms of the colonial troops were the same in all the French colonies in America after 1716-1718. The private soldiers wore a grey-white coat with blue cuffs and lining; blue waistcoat, breeches, and stockings; brass buttons; black tricorn hat laced with false gold; white cravat; shirt of "roussi" cloth; shoes with "two soles"; a pair of white duck gaiters; and sword and cartridge box belts of buff leather with brass buckles. They carried a leather (probably reddish-brown) cartridge box holding only nine cartridges, its flap bearing either the arms of the King engraved in leather or white leather anchor and border. Various types of powder horns were used,[5] and a sword with a brass hilt was carried in a brass-tipped scabbard. The uniform of the corporals was the same with the addition of a yellow woolen lace strip around their cuffs.[6] A grey-white watch coat was issued for sentry duty at Louisbourg. The *Cadets a l'Equillette* wore the same uniforms as the soldiers but with a distinctive shoulder knot or aiguillette of blue and white silk with brass-bound tips.[7]

Sergeants had the same uniform as privates but of better quality. The buttons were gilded; the hat lace was of fine gold; and the rank badge was an inch-wide fine gold lace border around each cuff. Sergeant-majors wore two lace stripes plus two more around each pocket flap. Sergeants were armed with a halberd and sword with a gilded brass hilt in a gilt-tipped scabbard.

Drummers wore the King's "small" livery. The coat was blue with red or scarlet cuffs, red lining, and ornamented with the King's livery lace (white chain on a crimson ground); red waistcoats, breeches, and stockings; and brass buttons. Other items were the same as those privates wore. Both the buff leather sword belt and drum belt had a livery lace border. Only one description of a drum has been found: in 1744, drum cases sent to Louisbourg were painted blue and sprinkled (surely with yellow) fleurs-de-lis.[8]

French officers in the 18th century wore the uniform of their unit but of better materials. Officers in Canada in 1731 requested that uniforms be provided them. This request was approved by the Minister of the Navy in 1732.[9] Presumably, the other colonies followed this precedent. These uniforms followed the style described above, being of the same color as those worn by the soldiers but of better quality cloth, with gold buttons, gold hat lace, and gilt gorget. The waistcoat was often laced with gold, but the coat was always free of lace. Officers' arms were a gilt-hilted sword and an espontoon.

In the western outposts of Canada such as Michilimackinac and probably Louisiana, uniforms were at first sent to the garrisons, but this proved too expensive.[10] As a result, soldiers who were sent to these posts clothed themselves with trade and Indian goods. Thus an officer at the battle of Monongahela in 1755 was clothed in buckskins with only a gorget to indicate his rank.[11] On campaign, the troops in Canada were

Soldier

Soldiers
[summer dress]

Soldier
[Western outposts]

Cadet 'a l'Eguillette   Sergeant   Officer   Drummer

French Colonial Infantry, 1740-1763

issued a "capot," two cotton shirts, a woolen blanket, cloth to make some "mitasses," a wool bonnet, buckskin breeches, and a portage collar, supplemented in winter by a sealskin, a pair of snowshoes, two pairs of moccasins, and two pairs of socks. Sergeants and officers left their halberds and espontoons behind and were armed with muskets.[12] In late 1754, the Louisiana companies replaced their bayonets with more useful small hatchets.[13] In Canada, while hatchets were also popular, the virtues of the bayonet were appreciated. Captain Pierre Pouchot reports that woodcutters' knives were used at Niagara in 1759 by those who did not have bayonets.[14]

The *Cannoniers-Bombardiers* cannoneers wore a blue coat with red cuffs and lining; red waistcoat, breeches, and stockings; white metal buttons; black tricorn hat laced with false silver; with other items as in the infantry. They carried a brass-hilted saber in a brass-tipped scabbard; sword knot of red, white, and blue mixed; buff leather belts with brass buckles; a cartridge box holding nineteen cartridges and bearing on its flap the arms of the King over two crossed anchors, engraved and inlaid with silver. Corporals wore the same uniform but used scarlet cloth instead of red; silvered buttons and silver hat lace. A strip of silver lace around the cuff designated their rank. Sergeants had two silver lace stripes around the cuff, and their saber hilts and scabbard tips were gilded; the sword knot was red, silver, and blue mixed. Drummers wore the King's small livery described above with white metal buttons, false silver hat lace, and a saber similar to the cannoneers'. All the enlisted ranks were issued a blue surtout which had a dozen white metal buttons; the drummers' also had livery lace on the sleeves. While servicing the piece, the men took off their coats and accouterments for ease of movement. Only the officers remained fully dressed. Officers wore the same uniform as the men but of better quality. Buttons were silver with a thin border and a rosette at the center. Their "half beaver" hats were laced with silver.

The uniform style shown in these plates is based on illustrations of French Navy and Army troops as they appeared in the middle of the 18th century. One notable detail about the colonial uniform is the lack of a collar on the coat. This is not mentioned in any of the clothing lists consulted, and it was not until 1759 that collars were added to colonial uniforms.[15]

Muskets generally resembled the 1728 Army model except that the barrel was fastened by pins. Army muskets may also have been used, since Captain Pouchot noted in 1755 that "the refuse arms of all the king's arsenals had been sent to this country. It was the same with the artillery, the cannon being all damaged by rust."[16]

Eugene Leliepvre
René Chartrand

The references upon which these plates are based are far too numerous to cite here. They cover several series of the French *Archives des Colonies* (henceforth cited as AC) over a 30-year period, besides the material from other sources. All archival documents cited are from microfilm or transcripts held by the Public Archives of Canada.

[1]They were also referred to as *Troupes de la Marine, Troupes de la Colonie*, and even *Regiment de la Marine*, which has resulted in much confusion. The ministry of Navy also maintained another type of *Compagnies Franches de la Marine* which were based in French seaports and served on board warships as marines.

[2]*Archives de la Guerre*, A1, 3573, No. 166; AC, B, 116, fol. 584; M. Bossu. *Nouveaux voyages dans l'Amerique*. Amsterdam, 1777. pp. 14, 17, 370.

[3]Moreau de Saint Mery. *Loix et constitutions des colonies francoises de l'Amerique sous le vent*. Paris: 1784-1790. Vol. IV, p. 454; and *Description topographique, physique, civile, politique et historique de la partie francaise de l'Isle de Saint Dominique*. Philadelphia: 1797. p. 484.

[4]AC, C11A, 56. p. 28; C11G, 12. p. 302; B. 54, fol. 338; 66. fol. 368; 92. fol. 449; Lemau de la Jaisse, *Septieme abrege de la carte generale du militaire de France sur terre et sur mer pour 1740*. Paris: 1741. 3rd pt., pp. 94-95.

[5]AC, C11A, 98, fol. 239; C11B, 31, p. 142.

[6]AC, C11A, 98, fol. 239. The corporals in Louisbourg had no distinctions on their uniforms despite the requests of the officials. C11B, 31, p. 142.

[7]AC, B, 55, fol. 96; 58, fol. 96v. Rochefort Archives. 11, 117, fol. 269.

[8]AC, F1, 35, fol. 10.

[9]*Bulletin dès recherches historiques*, XXII (1916), 353; AC, B, 57, fol. 629.

[10]*Rapport de l'archiviste de la Province de Quebec, 1921-1922*, pp. 198-199.

[11]AC, B, 72, fol. 391; Francis Parkman. *Montcalm and Wolfe*, Toronto; 1899, Vol. 1, p. 223.

[12]*Public Archives of Canada*, MG 18, 19, Vol. 3 (Papers of Chevalier de la Pause).

[13]George F. G. Stanley. *New France, the Last Phase, 1744-1760*. Toronto: Oxford Univ. Press. 1968. p. 78.

[14]Pierre Pouchot. *Memoir upon the Late War in North America, Between the French and English, 1755-60*. Roxbury, Mass.: W. E. Woodward, 1866. Vol. 1, p. 196; Sieur de Courville. *Memoire sur le Canada depuis 1749 Jusqu'a 1760*. Quebec: 1838. p. 180.

[15]AC, B, 110, fol. 540.

[16]Pouchot, *Ibid.* Vol. 1, 37; AC, C11a, 98, fol. 73. Naval artillery pieces were used in coastal forts.

Cannoneer, under arms   *Officer*   *Sergeant*   *Gun Crew*

French Colonial Artillery, 1740-1763

THE REVOLUTIONARY WAR PERIOD, 1770-1783

British Regular Units

British Provincial Units

German Units

Continental Units

State Units

French Units

29th Regiment of Foot, 1770

By 1770, public sentiment in Boston had developed into bitterness against the two British regiments which had been quartered in the Massachusetts capital for several years. Although the troops were, for the most part, well behaved, the open hostility of the Bostonians was so great that the soldiers could do little which would please the populace. The inevitable collision occurred on March 5, 1770 when a crowd gathered at the Customs House on King Street — now known as the old State House — to harrass the sentry. At his call, Captain Thomas Preston and seven men of the 29th Foot came to his aid. Name calling and rock-throwing goaded the soldiers into firing into the mob and five "patriots" were killed. The men of the 29th were arrested by the Crown.

In the trial of the soldiers, John Adams made a plea in their defense stating, "Every snowball, oyster shell, cake of ice, or bit of cinder that was thrown that night at the sentinel, was an assault upon him; every one that was thrown at the part of soldiers, was an assault upon them, whether it hit any of them or not."[1] Adams described the attack upon the soldiers in detail and in such a convincing manner that the jury acquitted the defendants, but the Regiment had earned the nickname of "the vein openers" and the Boston Massacre had become history.[2]

This plate shows the Regiment as it probably appeared on that unfortunate night. Their clothing would have been basically that prescribed by the Royal Warrant of 1768.[3] The Regimental distinctions were yellow facings and lapels, with silver metal for the officers and white lace with two blue and one yellow stripe for the corporals and privates. An inspection return of 1773 mentions that the hats were "ill-cocked," which suggests that the hats were cocked after an earlier fashion.[4]

Contemporary portraits of two officers of the Regiment indicate that the buttonholes of the officers' coats were neither laced nor embroidered.[5] For this reason, the officer in the plate has plain buttonholes.

The grenadier wears cloth gaiters with white metal buttons, a Regimental peculiarity at this time, and leather tops. Above the tops can be seen the stockings which were worn over the breeches when boots or gaiters were worn. It would appear that this was done in order to protect the knees of the breeches from being worn by any possible chafing. The laced cloth flaps on the shoulders of the coat were known as "wings." In the British service they had become the mark of the elite units such as grenadier and light infantry companies and were also worn by musicians.

The pioneer wears his distinctive cap, apron, and accouterments. His cap, though similar in shape to those of the grenadiers and drummers, actually had a leather crown. The front plate was of white metal with a red ground, above which was the bearskin trim which gave it its height. In addition to the usual infantry weapons, he carried a saw and an axe, carried in special scabbards or pockets suspended from narrow shoulder straps. The axe was carried on the left side.

Perhaps the most unusual Regimental distinction were the black drummers. Originally these were "eight or ten boys" who had been purchased as a gift to a former Regimental commander by his brother, Admiral Edward Boscawen, who bought the blacks in 1759 after the surrender of Guadaloupe. John Enys, who later commanded the Regiment, stated that when he joined in 1775, at least three of the original ten blacks were still active.[6] The custom of using black drummers was continued by the 29th Foot until well into the 19th century. The drummer wears "reversed colors" — in this case, a yellow coat faced with red — as was customary in most armies of this period. The front of the wooden drum is painted yellow, the Regiment's distinctive color.

Peter F. Copeland
Donald W. Holst

[1] *The Trial of the British Soldiers of the 29th Regiment of Foot . . . March 5, 1770.* Boston: William Emmons, 1824.

[2] The episode is described at some length, and from the regimental point of view, in Major Hugh E. E. Everard. *History of the 29th (Worcestershire) Foot 1694-1891.* Worcester: 1891. pp. 62-70. Unless otherwise noted, this history is the basic source for the plate, which has been produced with the cooperation of the Smithsonian Institution, Museum of History and Technology.

[3] In the celebrated engraving of the event made contemporaneously by Paul Revere, the soldiers are shown in what appears to be the pre-1768 uniform, with belts worn outside the coats, patches on the cuffs, voluminous skirts, etc. This has led subsequent artists like Howard Pyle to go even further astray. Actually there is no positive evidence that new clothing of the 1768 pattern had arrived in America by March 1770, although a glance at inspection returns for other British regiments suggests the issues were promptly made. See: Percy Sumner. "Army Inspection Returns — 1753 to 1804." Pt. 2. *Journal of the Society of Army Historical Research*, Vol. IV, January-March 1925. pp. 23, 37; and Pt. 3, *The Journal of the Society of Army Historical Research*, Vol. IV, April-June 1925, p. 115. Everard does not question the fact that the clothing and accouterments worn in March 1770 were according to regulation.

[4] Everard, *Ibid.* p. 73.

[5] *Ibid.* p. 91.

[6] *Ibid.* p. 55. Ten black drummers were reported at an inspection in April 1774. See: Sumner, Pt. 3, *Ibid.* p. 115. One of them Thomas Walker, was described in 1770 as a "big man"; he was active in roughing up the Bostonians and got bloodied as a result. See: John W. Shy. *Toward Lexington; the Role of the British Army in the Coming of the American Revolution.* Princeton: Princeton Univ. Press, 1965. p. 317.

29th Regiment of Foot, 1770

Light Company, 4th (King's Own) Regiment of Foot, 1774-1776

While some notable experiments with provisional light infantry units had been made during the Seven Years' War — better known in America as the "French and Indian War" — it was not until 1770 that the British Army began adding permanent light infantry companies to its regular infantry battalions. Because these companies were intended for skirmishing and other open-order work, it was obvious that they would require a less restrictive uniform than that worn by the grenadier and battalion companies. They were uniformed in a short coatee, red waistcoat, calf-length gaiters, and a leather cap. A grey shepherd's plaid was issued instead of a blanket or greatcoat. The light companies also received a lighter, shorter musket and a hatchet as well as a bayonet. All belts were to be inconspicuous, tanned leather. Their cartridge boxes, attached to the front of their waist belts, held nine cartridges. In addition, they carried powder horns and bullet pouches suspended from their right shoulders. The intent apparently was for the light infantryman to load with "loose" powder and ball while firing at will against individual targets, saving their nine cartridges for rapid volley fire. However, there was considerable variation in the types of cartridge boxes used by different regiments.

Some regimental commanders also took additional liberties with the regulations issued in 1771. Colonel Studholme Hodgson of the 4th Foot was evidently one of these. An inspection return of 1774 shows that the light company men had hats — not caps — bound with a scalloped lace. Moreover, their belts were not according to regulation, being white. The same return shows that this company used a German post horn for signalling. Officers also wore hats as is shown by a portrait executed about 1780, after the Regiment's return to England. In this case, however, the silver lace is not scalloped.

By the clothing warrant of 1768, the King's Own, as a Royal Regiment, had blue facings. All metal worn by the officers was silver. The men's lace was white with a blue stripe, looped square. Existing specimens of pewter buttons contain a Roman "IV" within a wreath border. A rectangular belt plate owned by Company of Military Historians Member Harry Trowbridge also has the "IV" engraved on it but has no other decoration whatsoever. Buttons and belt plates of officers followed a similar pattern, according to the above mentioned portrait of 1780. A subaltern's epaulette is shown in the portrait of another officer, painted about 1771.

This plate shows how the 4th Regiment's light company might have appeared during its tour of duty in Boston. It had arrived with the Regiment in mid-1774, and was subsequently detached for such actions as Lexington-Concord and Breed's Hill the following year. It embarked in January 1776, as one of the two light companies assigned to accompany Sir Henry Clinton to the seige of Charleston, South Carolina. In late 1778, the 4th Regiment was one of the ten regiments sent to the West Indies.

Perhaps it was during the dreary seige of Boston that someone carved the rather large, ornate powder horn carried by the officer. Powder horns and shot bags fell into general disuse during the course of the war and were officially abandoned in 1784.

Eric I. Manders

[1]The following references were taken from the *Journal of the Society of Army Historical Research:* Percy Sumner. "Army Inspection Returns — 1753 to 1804." Vol. IV, January-March, 1925. p. 33; W. Y. Baldry. "Light Infantry Clothing, 1771." Vol. XV, Winter 1936. pp. 249-250; H. Y. Usher. "Powder Horn, 4th Foot." Vol. XVIII, Spring 1939. p. 53.

Other References: Charles M. Lefferts. *Uniforms of the American, British, French, and German Armies in the War of the American Revolution, 1775-1783.* New York: New York Historical Society, 1926. pp. 152-153, 182-204; Cecil C. P. Lawson. *History of the Uniforms of the British Army.* London: Norman Military Publications, 1961. Vol. III, pp. 71-75, 109-120, 225; William Y. Carman. *British Military Uniforms from Contemporary Pictures.* London: Leonard Hill, 1957. pp. 96-98; William L. Calver and Reginald P. Bolton. *History Written with Pick and Shovel.* New York: New York Historical Society, 1950. pp. 49, 100, 110, 118; Sir Henry Clinton. *The American Rebellion; Sir Henry Clinton's Narrative of His Campaigns, 1775-1782.* New Haven: Yale Univ. Press, 1954. p. 24.

Music   Lieutenant   Private

Light Company, 4th (King's Own) Regiment of Foot, 1774-1776

35th Regiment of Foot, 1777-1778

One of the first British units sent to North America after Braddock's defeat in the French and Indian War, the 35th Regiment of Foot took part in the desperate defense of Fort William Henry and suffered from the subsequent massacre of captives by the French Indian allies. It revenged itself, however, in the capture of Louisbourg and particularly at Quebec. It was indeed ironic that the 35th Foot was returned to North America in 1775 to fight the very colonists whom it had earlier defended.

Arriving in Boston in early June 1775, the Regiment joined British forces in the battle of Bunker Hill; here its two flank companies suffered heavy losses. The 35th moved to New York and participated in the battles of Long Island and White Plains. In the latter engagement, its commander, Lieutenant Colonel Robert Carr, was fatally wounded. The Regiment was then detailed for garrison duty in the New York area where it served with no major combat role until 1778 when it joined British forces in the capture of St. Lucia in the West Indies.[1]

Since its raising at Belfast in 1701, the Regiment had worn the orange facings conferred on it by William of Orange.[2] Because of the inability to produce a pure orange dye economically, or as the result of dying unbleached material, the color appeared on the uniform as more of a brownish-yellow.[3] The clothing warrant of 1768 ordered white small clothes and coat linings, and silver appointments for officers. The white worsted lace, looped square, had a single yellow stripe.[4] Enlisted men's buttons were pewter, milled on the edges, and displaying the numeral 35.[5]

Drummers wore an orange coat faced with red and probably laced profusely in the style of the day. Their caps were black bearskin, like a grenadier's hat, except that the front plate displayed a trophy of colours and drums. They carried a scimitar-bladed short sword. The wooden drums were painted orange in front, with the crown and cypher over the Regimental number.[6]

The omission of the "Roussillon Plume" from the uniforms shown in this plate was made reluctantly, and only after a long search failed to uncover a contemporary mention of this distinctive item of dress. The story of the "Plume" is a colorful one.

At the Battle of Quebec in September 1759, the 35th held the right flank of Wolfe's line; there it met and defeated the Royal Roussillon Regiment posted on Montcalm's left. The men of the 35th then plucked the white plumes from the hats of their French prisoners and planted them in their own, thus establishing a tradition which lasted for some forty years. They also captured Roussillon's colours — bearing the golden *fleur-de-lis* — and, through the association of this insignia with their Regiment's orange facings, acquired the nickname "The Orange Lilies."[7]

Documents of the 18th century, however, tend to contradict the Roussillon Plume tradition by either inference or omission. French sources, for example, indicate that the Royal Roussillon probably wore a black cockade in 1759, not the white plume. French grenadiers often sported feathers in their bearskin caps, but there is no evidence that the Roussillon wore such caps in Canada.[8] Furthermore, British inspection returns for 1768-1770, 1778, and 1790 do not mention a plume for the 35th Regiment of Foot.[9]

Eric I. Manders

[1]Gerard D. Martineau. *A History of the Royal Sussex Regiment.* Chichester: Moore & Tillyer, 1953. *passim*; Richard Trimen, *An Historical Memoir of the 35th Royal Sussex Regiment of Foot.* Southhampton: 1873; *A Short History of the Royal Sussex Regiment (35th Foot-107th Foot) 1701-1926.* Aldershot: 1927.

[2]Martineau. *Ibid.*

[3]Cecil C. P. Lawson. *A History of the Uniforms of the British Army.* London: Norman Military Publications, 1961. Vol. III, pp. 118-119. The brownish yellow appearance may also have been caused by the ravages of time on the few pieces of evidence passed down to us.

[4]Charles M. Lefferts. *Uniforms of the American, British, French, and German Armies in the War of the American Revolution, 1775-1783,* New York: New York Historical Society, 1926. p. 192; also Lawson, *Ibid.*, pp. 91, 119, 256.

[5]William L. Calver and Reginald P. Bolton. *History Written with Pick and Shovel.* New York: New York Historical Society, 1950. pp. 10, 112, 113.

[6]Lefferts. *Ibid.* pp. 182, 185-186; Lawson, *Ibid.* pp. 110, 112-113. Clothing Warrant of 1768.

[7]Martineau. *Ibid.* p. 60; *Short History . . .*, *Ibid.* p. 5.

[8]W. Jacques Steeple and Henri Diard. *The Royal Roussillon: Notes on the History of a Famous French Regiment.* Unpublished MS dated January 1959, in the collection of Mr. Steeple, London.

[9]Percy Sumner. "Army Inspection Returns — 1753 to 1804." *The Journal of the Society of Army Historical Research.* Pt. 5, Vol. IV, October-December 1925, p. 172.

Drummer   Sergeant   Battalion and Light Company Men

35th Regiment of Foot, 1777-1778

Grenadier Company, 38th Regiment of Foot, 1775-1776

One of the first British units to be sent from Ireland, the 38th Foot arrived in Boston in either July or August 1774.[1] Its service for the next eight months consisted chiefly of constant training, guard duty, and various garrison chores. An occasional practice march into the countryside provided a break in garrison monotony. Lieutenant John Barker stated: "The Regt. march'd into the Country to give the Men a little exercise: this has been practised several days past by the Corps off duty; as they march with Knapsacks and Colours the People of the Country were allarm'd the first day, think those troops were sent out to seize some of the disaffected People; finding that is not the case they are since grown very insolent."[2]

When the decision was made to seize and destroy supplies and arms reportedly stored at Lexington and Concord, the grenadier and light infantry companies of the British regiments in Boston were detached and formed into a unit under Lieutenant Colonel Francis Smith. This was common practice throughout the war; the grenadier company of the 38th Foot became part of the 1st Grenadier Battalion under Colonel Meadows in late 1775 and thereafter served apart from its Regiment.[3]

The march to Lexington began on the night of April 18 and the British moved on to Concord the next morning. After arriving in Concord, the grenadiers were ordered to destroy some captured arms and supplies. The light infantry, meanwhile, moved to the bridge north of the village. "During this time," according to Barker, "the People were gathering together in great numbers and, taking advantage of our scatter'd disposition, seemed as if they were going to cut off the communication with the Bridge . . ."[4] Smith sent the grenadiers to their support and the combined force began to fall back under fire from "the People."

"We set out upon our return;" Barker continued, "before the whole had quitted the Town we were fired on from Houses and behind Trees, and before we had gone half a mile we were fired on from all sides, but mostly from the Rear, where People had hid themselves in houses till we had passed, and then fired . . ."[5] The British troops continued their retreat under heavy fire until they met reinforcements which assisted their return to Boston. The grenadier company of the 38th Foot lost four "rank and file" killed, twelve men and one officer wounded.[6]

As a part of Meadow's Grenadier Battalion, the company also fought at Bunker Hill. It is possible that this is the company portrayed by John Trumbull in his painting of the battle.

The uniforms shown in this plate are based in general upon the Royal Warrant of 1768. The lace worn by the 38th Foot was red, white, and yellow, its form being that of a "bastion loop." Distinctive regimental laces made it easy to distinguish soldiers of one regiment from another unit with the same color of facings, those of the 38th from the men of the 29th, for example. The soldiers in the plate are in normal field uniform and wear low spatterdashes instead of the higher black leggings used for parade. Their grenadier caps are based upon existing specimens described as having been worn in 1775-1776.

The coats of the officers of the 38th Foot were lappelled in the same style as those of the men but had silver-laced button holes. Silver epaulets were worn on each shoulder by both grenadier and light infantry officers; both also wore silver gorgets emblazoned with the King's arms and the regimental number. Their sword hilts were also of silver, and they wore crimson silk sashes fastened around their waists.

Grenadier coats had "wings" with six loops of the regimental lace. Sergeants wore crimson worsted sashes with a stripe of the color of the regimental facing; they carried a fusil instead of the halberd of infantry companies. Corporals wore a silk epaulet — actually pleated cords more like an aiguillette — on their right shoulder. Grenadiers carried short, slightly-curved cutting swords as a secondary weapon at the beginning of the war. These were gradually discarded, with only the sergeants retaining the sword as an additional indication of their grade.

The variation in the color of the coats shown was largely the result of different types of cloth and dye-stuffs. While red, often termed "scarlet", was the official color of British infantry coats, the privates' and corporals' coats were usually "brick" red. Sergeants' coats, made of "sergeants' cloth" of better quality, took the dye better and were brighter in color. Officers provided their own uniforms and could thus really blaze in scarlet although they might wear plain coats without lace on campaign. There was also considerable variation among the various regiments, depending upon their colonels' attitudes and the clothing materials available.

H. Charles McBarron, Jr.
George S. Pappas
John R. Elting

[1]"The Diary of Lieutenant John Barker, Fourth (or The King's Own) Regiment of Foot, From November, 1774, to May, 1776," *Journal of the Society of Army Historical Research*, Vol. VII, April 1928. p. 83; Vol. VII, Spring 1937. pp. 3-23.

[2]*Ibid.* p. 88.

[3]Lefferts, Charles M. *Uniforms of the American, British, French, and German Armies in the War of the American Revolution, 1775-1783.* New York: New York Historical Society, 1926. pp. 175-192.

[4]Barkley. *Ibid.* p. 99.

[5]*Ibid.* pp. 99-100.

[6]Frank Warren Coburn. *The Battle of April 19, 1775 in Lexington, Concord . . . Massachusetts.* Lexington: The Author, 1912, p. 159.

Company Officer   Sergeant   Grenadier

Grenadier Company, 38th Regiment of Foot, 1775-1776

42nd (Royal Highland) Regiment of Foot, (The Black Watch), 1784

This Regiment, which had already spent several years in North America during the French and Indian Wars, returned in May 1776, and served throughout the American Revolution. It was transferred to Nova Scotia in 1783 and returned to England in 1789.[1]

The plate shows the dress of the 42nd in 1784 after they arrived in Halifax. The rigors of campaigning in North America had effected a drastic change in their uniform: their kilts and plaids had been discarded and trousers and gaiters substituted. The Inspection Return of 1784 states that:

> The 42nd could not appear in their full uniform for want of plaids, etc., which the C. O. thought proper annually to dispose of during the late War, to purchase a more commodious dress for the American service, with the approbation of the Commander-in-Chief. The regiment appeared remarkably clean dressed — the men had on white strong ticken trousers with short, black cloth gaiters.[2]

Whether this change in uniform was because trousers and gaiters were better clothes for campaigning in North America as suggested, or whether the plaids and kilts simply wore out and could not easily be replaced cannot be determined. There is also a book, printed in New York in 1783, listing the British officers and regiments in North America in which someone wrote the facing colors beside each regimental designation. Alongside the 42nd is written: "Scott or Highland dress formerly, at present the same as the British regiments of Infantry that have short coats, except that they continue to wear the bonnet."[3]

In general, the uniform follows the clothing warrants of 1768. The coat is the short-skirted coat, faced blue and lined with white, bastion-shaped lace with one red stripe, and pewter buttons.[4] The belts and accouterment straps were black. Most, if not all, of the Regiment had discarded their broadswords by this time, but these are shown on the piper and officer since these individuals might have retained them out of national pride and as indicative of their rank. The scabbards had brass or copper-gilt mounts.[5] The Regiment had received Royal authority in 1773 to continue wearing the sash across the left shoulder.[6] Until approximately 1780, the cartridge box was worn in front on the waist belt; after that, there was a gradual transition to shoulder belts.[7]

The officer's uniform is taken from a portrait of Lieutenant James Stewart of the 42nd Regiment painted about 1780.

The dancer's shoes are Indian moccasins which are worn as a substitute to the "cuaran", a laced, heel-less shoe of untanned cowhide or deerskin used in the highlands, as much better for dancing than the regular issue shoe.[8]

The coat of the left-handed piper is a matter of conjecture. No descriptions of pipers' uniforms of the 42nd have been found. Drummers and fifers of Royal Regiments wore red coats faced blue and laced with Royal lace.[9] The piper is dressed in this manner but without the lace. The scarcity of descriptions of any pipers' uniforms leads one to suspect that the pipers were dressed according to the colonel's discretion. Inasmuch as they were used for morale building, rather than to give orders on the march or battlefield, there would be no need to dress them in the conspicuous manner of drummers. The third drone began to appear on the pipes about 1760.[10]

Eric I. Manders
George A. Snook

[1]C. T. Atkinson. "British Forces in North America, 1774-1781." *Journal of the Society of Army Historical Research.* Vol. XIV, Spring 1937, p. 7.

[2]Percy Sumner. "Army Inspection Returns, 1753-1804." *Journal of the Society of Army Historical Research.* Vol. V, January-March 1926, pp. 26-27.

[3]"An Officer of the Black Watch in the American Revolution." *Journal of the Society of Army Historical Research.* Vol. XXVI. Summer 1948, p. 78.

[4]Cecil C. P. Lawson. *A History of the Uniforms of the British Army.* Vol. III. London: Kaye & Ward, 1961. pp. 109-114.

[5]*Journal of the Society of Army Historical Research.* Vol. XIII, Autumn 1934, p. 176.

[6]Charles M. Lefferts. *Uniforms of the American, British, French, and German Armies in the War of the American Revolution, 1775-1783.* New York: New York Historical Society, 1926. p. 164.

[7]John T. Dunbar. *History of the Highland Dress.* Philadelphia: Dufour, 1964. p. 174.

[8]I. H. Mackay Scobie. "The Highland Independent Companies of 1745-1747." *Journal of the Society of Army Historical Research.* Vol. XX, Spring 1941. p. 37.

[9]Lawson. *Ibid.* p. 112.

[10]Dunbar. *Ibid.* p. 173.

42nd (Royal Highland) Regiment of Foot (The Black Watch), 1782

84th (Royal Highland Emigrants) Regiment of Foot, 1775-1783

There recently passed through our hands a manuscript ledger kept by the Regiment of Royal Highland Emigrants between 1761 and 1783. Much can be learned from these accounts about the administration of a British regiment of the Revolutionary War period, its clothing, subsistence and stores. For example, here is a copy of one page which shows the clothing and accouterments sold Major John Small, second-in-command, at Halifax in 1776:

Major John Small

Item	Price			
To 1-12/16 yeards scarlet cloath	at 21/p.yd.	1	16	9
¼ yard blue D°	20/		5	
14/16 yard white D°	20/		17	6
3½ yards Shalloon	2/		7	
2¾ yards damatty	3/6		9	7½
1 ounce white brown thread	1/6		1	6
1 oz. sewing silk D°	4/		4	
½ oz. scarlet D° D°	4/		2	
¼ oz. white silk twist	4/		1	
1 yard buckram	2/6		2	6
10 yard gold looping lace	6/	3		
1 pair gold epulitts	30/	1	10	
3½ dozen big buttons	2/6		8	9
1½ doz. small D°	2/		3	
1 plaid & kilt belt		1	13	3
2 pair hose	2/6		5	
1 bonnet, feather, & cockade			4	2
1 sashe		2	2	
1 purse and belt		11	3	
1 fuzil, bayonet & sling		3	4	6
1 pistol & belt		1	7	
1 broad sword & shoulder belt		4	10	
1 gorget			12	
1 cartouch box & waist belt			15	
To 1 tent & Marquies, poles, pins				
Matits, Valeizes, weather ropes				
& c. compleat			19	2

A page similar to this is devoted to each of the 62 officers of the Regiment, from Lieutenant Colonel Allan Maclean to Ensign Robert Campbell and Surgeon Boyd. Strangely, the number and type of the items sold, and their prices, with the sole exception of tents, are exactly the same for all the officers. Colonel Maclean was given a "fuzil", just like Ensign Campbell's, while the Ensign's "pair of gold epulitts" cost just as much as his colonel's.

The Royal Highland Emigrants was embodied in 1775 and regimented in 1778. It was raised by Maclean principally from among the Scottish settlers in Nova Scotia, Quebec, and upper New York. Many of its men were former soldiers of Fraser's Highlanders or other Highland regiments of the French and Indian War. The arrival of 230 of them at Quebec in December, 1775 probably was the major factor in saving that town from the Americans. In 1779 the Regiment was placed on the regular establishment and given the number "84". It consisted of two battalions. Major Small, whose clothing is listed above, commanded the Second Battalion, while Maclean had the First.

All accounts agree that the men and officers were dressed and accoutered the same as the 42nd (Royal Highland) Regiment. However, the "purses" (sporrans) were made of raccoon's skin instead of badger's. The men carried half-basket hilted swords while the officers, in addition to the broadswords listed above, are said also to have had dirks.

It will be clear to students of Scottish military dress that much reliance has been placed on the drawing of an officer of the 42nd Regiment, 1780, by Edward Dayes, which was reproduced and described by Major I. H. Mackay Scobie in the *Journal of the Society of Army Historical Research*, Vol. XVII, 1838, pp. 1-2. The rather unusual purse shown by Dayes has been used as a basis for the Highland Emigrant officer's raccoon purse, and the square ended buttonholes have also been copied.

The purses of the men were doubtlessly plainer than those worn by officers. Dirks and broadswords at this period were not of special regimental patterns and no doubt other articles of clothing were free from strict regulation. The background figure shows it was quite possible to wear full equipment even with the belted plaid. With the cartridge box worn on the front of the waist, the haversack and canteen could be carried on the right hip to balance the broadsword and belted plaid.

There is an oil portrait of Small in the McCord Museum, McGill University, Montreal, and a miniature of him in the Museum of the City of New York. The 2nd Battalion's color is on display in the Canadian Public Archives Offices, Ottawa.

H. Charles McBarron, Jr.
Frederick P. Todd

Company Officer   Private Soldiers

84th (Royal Highland Emigrants) Regiment of Foot, 1775-1783

The Royal Navy, 1775-1783

The period covered by the American Revolution or, as we call it in England, the American War of Independence, was a time of transition for British naval uniforms. Officers' dress was becoming more standardized and was being more consistently worn. The days when an officer appeared on deck in a variation of civilian attire were over. The clothing regulations laid down definite cuts for the coats, and defined the lace to be worn by the various ranks.[1] Breeches and stockings were white as were the lapels and cuffs of the coat. The headgear was the tricorne with a black cockade on the left side. The hat was laced with gold according to rank, but not to indicate rank, e.g., a midshipman would wear no gold lace whereas an admiral's hat would be heavily laced.

Two items of the period do not appear to have been strictly regulated: stocks and cravats, and swords. The older generation, as today, tended to retain the fashion of its youth, while the younger officers adopted the new ideas. Thus we find the admiral still wearing the white stock and cravat, which was at this time superceded by an all black cravat over a white stand-up collar, which was completely or almost completely hidden. The midshipman in this plate wears such a collar — somewhat untidily! The captain, keeping to the middle of the road, favours a white cravat on a black stock. Swords were a matter of personal perference, though two types of sword seem to have been most generally used: the short "hunting sword" or curved military hanger, and the longer rapier-type colichemarde such as the sword held by the admiral in this plate. These swords carried a blue and gold sword knot. Wigs were still used by the older officers, but the younger men wore their own hair long and tied back in a queue.

The admiral's dress illustrated is taken from an all-purposes uniform coat and waistcoat, originally belonging to Admiral Sir James Douglas and still to be seen in the Scottish United Services Museum in Edinburgh Castle. This uniform was made after the flag-officers' full dress uniform was abolished in 1767 and replaced by the all-purposes uniform. The main changes from the earlier uniforms were narrower and shorter lapels, with the buttonholes horizontal. The extremely large, deep cuffs were replaced by much smaller boot cuffs, and the buttonholes were laced in a more open manner with a type of bastion loop. Though far less gold lace was used with this uniform, an admiral's coat, by modern standards, was still heavily laced — front, sides, and rear.

The captain is wearing a full dress uniform authorized in 1774. The changes made at that time merely consisted of adjustments to convert all-purpose uniforms to dress uniforms: blue breeches were changed to white and plain unlaced waistcoats were prescribed. An undress blue frock coat without facings also was authorized at this time. Lieutenants' uniforms were simpler, having narrower lapels and slashed cuffs without lace. The midshipmen's dress was first introduced in 1748, but there appears to be no official record of it until 1787, when a three-button round cuff is mentioned. The midshipman in this plate is based upon an aquatint published in 1777 which is now in the National Maritime Museum, Greenwich, England.

Seamen still had no uniform prescribed as such, although ships' captains might establish their own standards of dress. The seaman in this plate wears short, roomy trousers and what appears to be a leather boarding helmet. His neckerchief is the traditional sailor's black, a color that concealed stains from perspiration or tar.

Russell Gammage

---

[1] The first move to make naval officers' dress uniform was an order from the Lord High Admiral's Office, dated April 13, 1748, and signed by Duncannon, Earl of Sandwich. This directed that in future all officers should wear uniforms appropriate to their rank, and that patterns of such uniforms were held at the Admiralty Office. Subsequent changes were published in the *London Gazette* with the date of the order. The pertinent changes for this period were orders dated July 13, 1767 and January 23, 1768.

Admiral   Midshipman   Seaman   Captain

The Royal Navy, 1775-1783

11th New Hampshire Provincial Regiment, 1774-1775

Until 1773 the Province of New Hampshire's well-organized militia consisted of a "Regiment of Horse Guards" and nine infantry regiments. Most of the officers and men enrolled in these commands were veterans of the Seven Years' War.[1]

New Hampshire's last royal governor, John Wentworth, was a dedicated military buff who conscientiously discharged his concurrent duties as "captain general of militia." Late in 1773 he decided to strengthen his command and exerted his considerable personal influence to secure the authorization for three additional infantry regiments, designated the 10th, 11th, and 12th.[2] While his sense of timing may appear faulty in view of the political discontent then prevailing, he was not the only governor so interested. The British government, mindful that Pontiac's Rebellion might be only the first of a series of Indian wars, had been mildly hopeful that its colonies would improve their own military forces. At the same time, an effective militia, officered by loyal subjects, would greatly strengthen the King's authority in case of civil disturbance.

Little is known of these new regiments except the names of their colonels and the towns from which they were recruited.[3] Fortunately, some information as to the 11th Regiment is preserved in an old and obscure history of Concord, New Hampshire.[4] In addition to providing names of officers and non-commissioned officers, it also specifies the officers' uniform:

UNIFORM OF THE REGIMENT

The officers to wear red coats, cuff'd, lin'd and lapel'd with sky-blue. Sky-blue waistcoats and breeches, all trim'd with white. Black hats with silver hat-band, button and loops, without lace. White stockings, cocade, sash and white gorgets. Swords with silver hilts. Captains and Lieutenants to carry fusees. Field officers to wear silver shoulder knots.

By order of His Excellency,
John Wentworth, Esq., Captain-General
February 15, 1774.

In some respects, this uniform was old-fashioned for the Clothing Regulations of 1768 authorized the army's shift to white (sometimes buff) waistcoats and breeches. Epaulettes had replaced the earlier shoulder knots. Possibly Wentworth designed the 11th Regiment's uniform from his memories of earlier service.

There is no mention of any uniform for the enlisted men and no regimental muster rolls have yet been found. The composition of these companies, with townsmen, farmers, and seafaring men — and a sprinkling of the ubiquitous "free men of color" — in the ranks, would ensure a variegated appearance. Probably those enlisted men who had red civilian coats wore them on muster day. The sergeants undoubtedly provided themselves with a uniform of sorts. Halberds would be useful on ceremonial occasions, if only to get the men into something resembling a line.

Organized early in 1774, these new regiments had a short existence but provided patriotic citizens an opportunity to acquire a brief measure of military drill and experience. This was important; several of the officers and non-coms of the Concord companies appear on the muster rolls of units that fought at Bunker Hill, and Thomas Stickney, the Regiment's lieutenant colonel, distinguished himself at Bennington.[5]

The major of the 11th Regiment achieved distinction in another way. Benjamin Thompson was not quite twenty-one when he was commissioned by Governor Wentworth. Always the accomplished fop, Thompson is shown in this plate uniformed in the high pitch of contemporary style — beribboned shoes and double-breasted vest. Thompson had physical attractiveness, charm, and personality enough for a platoon. In his case, at least, Wentworth's ambition was achieved: Thompson served his King loyally as a spy until — after twice facing down charges of treason before public meetings of the Committee of Safety — he decided it was healthier to abandon his wife and child and defect to the British. He subsequently achieved distinction as an under-secretary of state and later as commander of the King's American Dragoon Regiment. Knighted in 1784, Thompson ended as a count of the Holy Roman Empire and a lieutenant general in the Bavarian Army.

Peter F. Copeland
James P. Simpson

[1]New Hampshire. Adjutant General's Office. Report 1866. Concord, N. H.: Vol. II, p. 258. In North America the Seven Years War was known as the French and Indian War.
[2]*Ibid.* pp. 260-261.
[3]*Ibid.* p. 261.
[4]Nathaniel Bolton. *The History of Concord.* Concord, N. H.: B. W. Sanborn, 1856. p. 257.
[5]Family papers of Mrs. Elma M. Simpson.

Privates

Company Officer   Major   Sergeant

11th New Hampshire Provincial Militia 1774-1775

The Queen's Rangers (1st American Regiment), 1778-1783

The Queen's Rangers came into being when Robert Rogers was authorized to raise a "Corps of Provincials" on August 16, 1776. Recruited originally from Loyalists in New York and Connecticut, its men were farmers and city dwellers with little military experience. Following an inauspicious start when it was mauled by an American surprise attack at Mamaroneck in October 1776, it participated successfully in various campaigns throughout the Revolution until the surrender at Yorktown.[1]

In a period of about a year, the Rangers had three commanding officers following Rogers. Major Christopher French reorganized the corps, during which process many officers and enlisted men were discharged. He was followed by Major James Wemyss in May 1777, under whom the unit increased in size and efficiency, participating in the Brunswick raid of June 1777. In the battle of Brandywine, the command suffered the loss of one-third of its number in killed or wounded; fourteen of twenty-one commissioned officers were casualties.

Wemyss was wounded at the battle of Germantown. Major John Graves Simcoe succeeded him as commanding officer on October 15, 1777. It was under Simcoe that the Rangers reached the height of its efficiency. Starting as an infantry command, it gradually expanded and before its surrender at Yorktown consisted of eleven companies of foot (including riflemen, light infantry, grenadiers, and a Highland company), dragoons, hussars, and some light guns.

Simcoe had advanced ideas regarding training and discipline. He advocated constant vigilance, physical activity, and endurance of fatigue. There was constant instruction in marksmanship, the use of the bayonet, open formations, and the use of ambuscades. The unit seldom returned by its outgoing route. Officers were selected for special duty on the basis of their ability to perform such duty. Promotions, when they occurred, were within the corps. Regularity of messing and cleanliness were stressed, and officers were held responsible for the health of their men. Written orders were avoided when possible; officers met after parade and received their orders verbally.

The British originally furnished their Provincial troops with green uniforms with various colored facings. These were replaced with red coats in 1778, but Simcoe was able to retain the green color for his Rangers. The uniforms shown in this plate are based upon several watercolors by Captain James Murray of the Rangers, preserved in the Toronto Central Library. They show the Rangers as they appeared after 1778.

The Hussar wears a dark-green coatee with green collar, cuffs, and shoulder straps. His breeches are dark-green and he wears black boots. His cap, or busby, is black felt with a green bag and a white tassel. On the front is a silver crescent. He is equipped with saber and pistol.

The Rifleman wears a short, green, sleeved waistcoat with white overalls. His leather cap has a black or green feather and the hackle is black with a white center. He carries a rifle and a powder horn.

The Grenadier wears a green coat with white lining and a green waistcoat. The wings are green, laced and edged with white. Breeches and stockings are white; and the short gaiters, black. His high fur cap has a silver crescent and a black-and-white plume. He carries a musket.

The Highlander wears a blue bonnet with a red-and-white diced band and a black plume. His coat is green and the tartan is MacNab. The sword belt and sporran are brown. In addition to his musket, he carries a broadsword and a dirk. His stockings are red and white.

The Light Infantryman wears the same leather cap as the Rifleman, but the feather at its crest is white; he also has a green hackle with a white center which is not visible in this position. His short, sleeved waistcoat is green, and he wears white breeches, stockings, and black gaiters.

The officer wears the Light Infantry cap with a black plume, a black-and-white hackle, and a black cockade. The coat and waistcoat are green, the former lined with white. Lace and buttons are silver, as is the epaulet. He wears a red sash, white breeches and stockings, and black gaiters. The spacing of his buttons and braid are based upon an officer's coat in the Fort York museum. He carries a fusil and a sword.

H. Charles McBarron, Jr.
Rutledge F. Smith

[1]John G. Simcoe. *Simcoe's Military Journal A History of the Operations of a Partisan Corps, called the Queen's Rangers* New York: Bartlett & Welford, 1844. Other useful accounts exist by Fellow John R. Cuneo, James Hannay, H. M. Jackson, George H. Locke, and the autobiography of Stephen Jarves, of Danbury, Conn., who served in the Rangers' calvalry.

Hussar

Light Infantry

Rifleman   Grenadier   Highlander   Officer

The Queen's Rangers (1st American Regiment), 1778-1783

The King's American Regiment of Foot (4th American Regiment), 1776-1783

The King's American Regiment of Foot was the brain-child and meal ticket of Edmund Fanning who was born on Long Island, graduated from Yale, and became a resident of North Carolina. There he practiced law and became a man of considerable note — although the exact nature of said note remains a matter of dispute. His appreciative heirs recalled ". . . the world did not contain a better man in all the various relations of life: as a husband, a parent, and a friend — as a landlord and a master, he was kind and indulgent." Lorenzo Sabine counters that he was "remarkable for all the vices which degrade the most abandoned and profligate minion."[1] It seems apparent, however, that he applied himself to one of his official positions — that of "Recorder of Deeds for the County of Orange" — with more industry than integrity, thereby helping bring on the "Regulator" troubles. At the outbreak of the Revolution, Fanning displayed notable initiative in evacuating himself to New York.

In December 1776, Fanning obtained a warrant to raise a Loyalist regiment initially dubbed "The Associated Refugees," but soon given the more ringing title, "The King's American Regiment."[2] The necessary funds for its activation were secured through subscriptions from active Royalists, some 3000 pounds being raised in and around New York City.

The King's American Regiment was a two-battalion unit raised "for the American service, and for the term of two years, or during the war, at the General's discretion."[3] Its initial strength seems to have been 460, all ranks. As with most Loyalist regiments, officers were easily secured but enlisted men were difficult to find.

The Regiment spent 1777 near New York City; the "state" of January 1, 1778 definitely shows it to be there. In August 1778, it was part of the British garrison of Rhode Island, having arrived there as part of the reinforcements sent to counter the bungled French-American attack on Newport. The Regiment returned to New York and remained there until October 1780 when it took part in diversionary raids in Virginia. It later was part of a force sent from Virginia to Charleston, South Carolina. From Charleston, it moved to Savannah and took part in operations in Georgia and eastern Florida where it was reported as somewhat celebrated for its spirited conduct in the field during the southern campaigns of 1780-1781. This service must have been strenuous for a "state" of September 1, 1781, showed the Regiment's strength reduced to 271.

This increased reputation may possibly be traced to the fact that Colonel Fanning remained in New York. The Regiment was commanded by Lieutenant Colonel George Campbell while in Charleston in August 1781. Fanning in 1782 was the Surveyor-General of New York, a post not likely to prove too dangerous.

In 1783, the King's American Regiment was placed on the regular British establishment as the 4th American Regiment. Fanning at once demanded — and received — a royal commission as colonel in the British regular service. For some reason, now imperceptible, he was well cared for thereafter, advancing in grade to general in 1808. His regiment was disbanded in Canada in 1783.

Loyalist uniforms are, if possible, even more of a puzzle than those of their American opponents. They began the war much in rags but were then uniformed in green faced with white, green or blue. Orange, red, and black were later added as facing colors. By 1778, most of the Loyalists seem to have had red coats although some light units, such as the Queen's Rangers and the British Legion, wore their original green throughout the war.[4] A manuscript "List of Officers of the Army Serving in North America . . . New York, 1783" describes the King's American Regiment's uniform as "Red coats with olive facings and variety buttonholes." The uniforms shown in the plate are taken from this period. The drummer's uniform is based on a note in the "Carleton Papers" that indicated that provincial drummers' coats were to be different colors based upon their regimental facings. Another list for 1783, possibly issued after the "regularization" of the Regiment, gives its facings as blue.

There are several unusual items of information available regarding the uniform of the Regiment — an officer's gilt gorget,[5] an officer's belt plate,[6] and several buttons.[7] The fact that the gorget and belt plate were of yellow metal indicates that the officers' "metal" and lace would be gold. While most Loyalist uniforms were of simple cut, the elaborate design of the gorget and belt plate, as well as Fanning's known character, would indicate that this Regiment's uniforms would tend toward the showy side.

The flank company officer's uniform is taken from a portrait in *Journal of the Society of Army Historical Research*, Winter 1949. The short, double-breasted waistcoat would be practical for field duty as would the shortened coattails and the heavy, curved sword. Although the ordinary cocked hat would be favored for off-duty wear, some sort of cap would have been worn for parade or battle. The major wears a regulation uniform, complete with ordinary dress sword.

Frederick Ray, Jr.
John R. Elting

[1]Lorenzo Sabine. *Biographical Sketches of Loyalists in the American Revolution*. Boston: Little, Brown, 1864.

[2]C. T. Atkinson. "British Forces in North America, 1774-1781." *Journal of the Society of Army Historical Research*. Vol. XVI, Spring 1937. pp. 3-23.

[3]George MacMunn. *The American War of Independence in Perspective*. London: G. Ball & Son, 1939. pp. 437-457.

[4]Charles M. Lefferts. *Uniforms of the American, British, French, and German Armies in the War of the American Revolution, 1775-1783*. New York: New York Historical Society, 1926. p. 222.

[5]H. Oakes Jones. "The Evolution of the Gorget." *Journal of the Society of Army Historical Research*. Vol. II, January 1923. pp. 22-31.

[6]Photograph furnished by Frederick P. Todd.

[7]William L. Calver. "Distinctive Buttons of the Loyalist Corps in the American Revolution." *New York Historical Society Quarterly Bulletin*. January 1929.

Private, Battalion
Company

Drummer

Flank Company
Officer

Major

-RAY-

The King's American Regiment of Foot (4th American Regiment), 1776-1783

Butler's Rangers, 1778-1784

On September 15, 1777 beating orders were issued to Maj. John Butler, authorizing him to enlist eight companies of rangers; each to have one captain, one lieutenant, three sergeants, three corporals and fifty privates. Two of the companies were to be formed of "people speaking the Indian language and acquainted with their customs and manner of making war," the men to get four shillings (New York currency), a day. The men of the remaining companies, "to be composed of people acquainted with the woods, in consideration of the fateague they are liable to undergo," were to receive two shillings a day.[1]

Before the war, Butler had been an officer of the Indian Department under Sir William Johnson. He left his Mohawk Valley home at the outbreak of hostilities and gathered about him a number of other Loyalist refugees, chiefly from his own Tryon County. These were with him before Fort Stanwix in 1777, and subsequently became the core of his outfit.

The Rangers were used principally for commando-like raids along the frontiers, concentrating on the grain fields of northern New York. As a body or in detachments, they took part in almost all the major actions of the Hudson-Delaware-Susquehanna border. Parties from Fort Niagara kept the Pittsburgh-Wheeling sector active, while another detachment at Detroit operated on the Ohio as far south as Kentucky. These were hard men with personal scores to settle with their former neighbors. They waged a bloody, no-quarter war, and were paid back in kind.

Six companies were assembled at Niagara in December 1778 to receive their clothing.[2] Lefferts devotes a plate to the corps; his text describes the dark green coats and waistcoats, scarlet facings, black leather caps, buff cross belts and leather overalls.[3] His brass cap plate, however, seems a bit oversize for a woods-running ranger outfit. Specimens of the cartridge box badge, sword belt plate and buttons have been unearthed by the New York Historical Society.[4]

The Iroquois costume at this period was of red and blue trader's broadcloth, decorated with beads and quills. A kilt was often worn in lieu of a breechclout, and the seams of the leggings ran up the front instead of the side.[5] The head-dress of Joseph Brant, painted in London in 1775 and shown here, is somewhat different from the horsehair roach usually depicted. The ubiquitous Indian sash worn by the Ranger officer is similar to the one worn by Superintendent Guy Johnson in the same portrait.[6] The Indians apparently regarded it as a badge of rank.[7]

It was intended that the battalion should be armed with rifles, but as each man was required to clothe and arm himself at his own expense, he brought with him any kind of firearm he could procure. The commandant at Niagara was often obliged to lend them firelocks from the magazine.[8]

Concerning their training, General Frederick Haldimand directed: "Rangers are in general separated, and the nature of their service little requires the forms of parade or the manoeuvres practised in the field. It is the duty, and I am persuaded will be the pleasure, of every captain to perfect his company in dispersing and forming expeditiously, priming and loading carefully, and levelling [aiming] well. These, with personal activity and alertness, are all the qualities that are effective or can be wished for in a ranger." In 1779 they were trained in the use of light fieldpieces.[10]

For the Schoharie campaign of 1780, it was directed that the troops at Niagara be "provided with a blanket, leggings and a pair of moccasins."[11] Describing the battle at Johnstown in 1781, Cruikshank says "The rangers began the action with a volley, which they followed up by charging with their well-known Indian yell."[12]

Butler was given permission to raise two more companies in 1781, and the corps was not disbanded until June 1784.[13]

Eric I. Manders

[1]Ernest A. Cruikshank. *The Story of Butler's Rangers*. Welland, Ontario: Tribune Printing Co., 1893. pp. 37-38. This is his principle work on the Corps. Also useful is Howard Swiggett. *War Out of Niagara*. New York: Columbia Univ. Press, 1933.

[2]Cruikshank. *Ibid*. p. 58. Apparently they were not in uniform at Wyoming or Cherry Valley in 1778.

[3]Charles M. Lefferts. *Uniforms of the American, British, French, and German Armies in the War of the American Revolution, 1775-1783*, New York: New York Historical Society, 1926. pp. 212-213. He says "a low, flat cap."

[4]W. L. Calver and R. P. Bolton, *History Written with Pick and Shovel* New York: New York Historical Society, 1950; photos on pp. 56, 129, 160, 168. The buttons have the words BUTLERS RANGERS embossed on them.

[5]Carrie A. Lyford, *Iroquois Crafts*, United States Department of the Interior, no date. pp. 25, 26.

[6]*The American Heritage Book of the Revolution*, New York, 1958. p. 317.

[7]Lyford, *Ibid*. p. 24.

[8]Cruikshank, *Ibid*. p. 59.

[9]Cruikshank, *Ibid*. pp. 78-79. He gives no date.

[10]Cruikshank, *Ibid*. p. 79.

[11]Cruikshank, *Ibid*. p.83.

[12]Cruikshank, *Ibid*. pp. 100-101.

[13]Cruikshank, *Ibid*. pp. 91, 97, 113.

Rangers and [Center] Company Officer

Butler's Rangers, 1778-1784

Loyal Queen's County Militia, 1780

Immediately after the battle of Long Island, the British command began the reorganization of the militia of Long Island and other portions of New York State under their control. On December 10, 1776, Governor William Tryon wrote Lord George Germain " . . . I reviewed the militia of Queens county at Hempstead, when 820 men were mustered: and on Tuesday following I saw the Suffolk militia at Brookhaven, where near 800 appeared, to all of whom, as well as the militia of Queens county, I had in my presence an oath of allegiance and fidelity administered . . ."[1]. On January 20, 1777, he reported that he had secured "800 stand of arms for the loyal inhabitants of Queens county."

To command the Queens County Militia, Archibald Hamilton, Esquire, "a Scottish gentleman" who claimed twenty-seven years' service in Flanders, America, and the West Indies, was commissioned lieutenant colonel. He was loyal to his King, and outspokenly so. Consequently, he was arrested, put in a common jail, and later sent to Philadelphia.[2] How he got back to New York does not appear, but Tryon found him available and, small wonder, willing.

Hamilton's orders for the organization of his new command were vigorous and complete. Queens County was divided into districts, each of them under a militia captain who was to keep an exact return of the number of men in it fit to bear arms. There would be regular field days which must be attended with "their arms complete. No excuse but want of health will be admitted." Loyal Quakers were to be shown "every lenity," but those who were "aiders or abettors of this unnatural rebellion were to be constantly warned to appear, and to be fined for non-compliance." Men were to be "clean and decent under arms." Also, they were to be sober on their way to drill and — far worse — on their way home. Any man "who shall neglect to appear when warned, or shall contumaciously refuse any lawful order, will not only be fined but sent to the Provost-guard."[3]

This Loyalist militia performed all sorts of duties, most of which involved coast watching and coastal defense against raiding American whaleboat parties. Many of them, like their colonel, had old grudges to pay off; the waters and shores of Long Island Sound were another "Debatable Ground," where many a savage squabble killed men without benefit of drum, trumpet or ordered line.

Vengeance aside, the duty had its drawbacks. Members of the militia had to contribute and deliver material, at their own expense, for the repair and expansion of British fortifications on Long Island. Furthermore, "the militia of Kings and Queens were obliged to act by rotation as labourers in building these forts, a certain number from each company being weekly employed upon this service . . . but not a single

sixpence by way of pay was allowed a soul of them. But what was still worse (if anything can be worse) the Colonels of the two counties, Aztell of Kings and Hamilton of Queens, fined all the defaulters who could not give a satisfactory reason for their non-attendance upon their respective terms of duty, and as the fines were the property of the two Colonels, few excuses were judged satisfactory . . . In case of refusal to pay the fine a militia officer was ordered to distrain, who in general took treble the value of the sum demanded. As the Colonel and his officers, the distrainers, were generally the bidders, nobody dared to bid above them, and the distrained goods were disposed of at about one-third of their real value."[4]

Hamilton, however, could sing his own song of woe. He received neither pay nor allowances. During his involuntary residence in Philadelphia, the 71st Foot had encamped on his farm "to the ruin of his walls and fencing, loss of cattle, etc." In December 1779, his house — which appears to have also served his regiment as a powder magazine — caught fire and was totally destroyed.[5]

The officers' uniforms shown here are taken from a regimental order of February 7, 1780:

> Colonel Hamilton desires that the officers of the Regiment of Loyal Queens County will provide themselves immediately each with a uniform or regimentals. It is to be scarlet, faced with blue, with white lining, white waistcoat and breeches, and silver buttons, with a silver epaulet, a well-cocked hat with silver buttons and loops and a silver hat band.[6]

Nothing is said about the men's clothing, except that it should be clean. The sergeant is shown with an improvised uniform coat and a home-made halberd. The weapons and equipment seem to have been whatever could be spared. In June of 1778, the Queens County men took over the muskets "with wooden ramrods" and the "old cartridge boxes" of DeLancey's Brigade.[7]

Frederick Ray, Jr.
John R. Elting
Henry I. Shaw, Jr.

[1] Henry Onderdonk. *Documents and Letters Intended to Illustrate the Revolutionary Incidents of Queens County.* New York: Leavitt, Trow & Co., 1846. p. 130.

[2] *Ibid.* p. 131.

[3] Henry Onderdonk. *Documents and Letters Indended to Illustrate the Revolutionary Incidents of Queens County.* Second Series. Hempstead, L. I.: Van de Water, 1884. p. 31.

[4] Thomas Jones. *History of New York During the Revolutionary War.* New York: New York Historical Society, 1879. Vol. I, p. 347-348.

[5] *Report on American Manuscripts in the Royal Institution of Great Britain.* London: 1904-09. Vol. IV, pp. 307-478.

[6] Onderdonk. Second Series. *Ibid.* pp. 43-44.

[7] *Orderly Book, DeLancey's Brigade.* pp. 99, 110.

Private   *Sergeant*   *Captain*   *Major*

Loyal Queen's County Militia, 1780

The Quebec Militia, 1775-1776

After the fall of New France, the British authorities kept basically the same militia organization which had previously fought against them. In the years of peace that followed, the militia remained inactive.[1] By 1775, the situation in the American colonies became of major concern to Canada, and on June 9, Governor Sir Guy Carleton declared martial law. The Canadians remained generally neutral to these events, although some joined the Americans as they invaded Canada while others remained loyal to the Crown.

In Quebec City, the militia consisted of six companies of English-speaking residents called the "British Militia," eleven companies of French-speaking "Canadian Militia," and an artillery company. All received arms on September 19. General Orders of the Quebec Garrison[2] provide some indication of the arms, clothing, and accouterments that they used. Officers were to appear with their side arms and cockades. Those who disliked the "large pouches" could exchange them for cartridge boxes. Orders for November 24 prescribe:

> A Sergeant of each company to receive a suit of clothes each. It is to be made up immediately & directly, to the Patron [Pattern] which Mr. McLeod, Taylor, will have ready tomorrow which will be a plain green coat, with buff waistcoat and Breeches. As there will not be green cloth sufficient to make cuffs and collars, Mr. McLeod will give as much green cloth as will serve that purpose.

Other orders directed officers to have "cloathing of the same & so made up, plain green with a cuff & collar a pattern of which Mr. McLeod will show." The men of the "Several Companies" now "thinly clad" were also to have this uniform made "as far as possible beginning with the oldest Company." Silver epaulettes were added to the officers' uniforms on December 12. Arms were English or French muskets until December 9 when it was announced that the British Militia were "all to receive new Arms," presumably the same as the regulars. By December, the Canadian Militia had been reorganized into eight companies.[3]

The services of the militia during the American seige of Quebec were numerous. They distinguished themselves during the final assault in the early morning hours of December 31, 1775, defending Cape Diamond where General Richard Montgomery was killed and participating in the house-to-house fighting which preceded General Benedict Arnold's retreat.

On May 22, 1776, the British and Canadian Militia units were dismissed from duty. Although they sometimes gathered for social occasions, such as the ball given on December 31, 1776, or were reviewed "under arms on the parade", these activities came to a stop with the end of the war.[4]

The officer in the plate wears a dark green coat with cuffs and collar of the same colour, white lining, silver epaulettes and buttons, buff vest and breeches as indicated by the above orders and by contemporary observers.[5] The usual distinctions of officers have been added: Crimson sash, silver gorget and sword hilt, with gold and crimson sword knot. The hat is laced with silver.

The private has the same uniform without the officer's distinctions. He has pewter buttons instead of silver, a hat laced with white, and armament similar to a British regular soldier.

Although winter clothing is not mentioned, it would appear each man furnished his own. Therefore, the militiaman in the center is dressed in typical Canadian winter garments. He wears a white "capot" trimmed with a dark blue band at the cuffs and around the skirt, and fastened with dark blue ribbons. His "mitasses" or leggings are of blue cloth and his moccasins of cowhide. The worsted sash is mostly red and his "tuque" or wool cap is red, indicating that the wearer is from the Quebec District.[6]

H. Charles McBarron, Jr.
Réne Chartrand

[1] It should be noted that a body of Canadian volunteers was raised in 1764 to help suppress Pontiac's uprising.

[2] Public Archives of Canada (PAC), C 1713, MS *Quebec Garrison, General Orders*, begun by Captain A. Vialar (British Militia) on September 17, 1775, and continued by Captain R. Lester (British Militia) from November 16, 1775.

[3] PAC, C 1714, MS *Nouveau Role de la Milice Canadienne, Ville de Quebec*, December 16, 1775. The eight companies in this list totaled 563 officers and men.

[4] *Quebec Gazette*, 1775 to 1784, passim.

[5] A German officer wrote on December 31, 1776: "All the gentlemen residing in Quebec wore, as officers de milice, a green uniform with straw-coloured facings, vests, and breeches, and silver epaulets." (Ray Pettengill, ed., *Letters from America, 1776-1779*, Port Washington, N.Y.: Kennikat Press, reprint edition, 1964, p. 58.) What the German most likely saw were uniforms made in 1776 after the siege was over and the supply situation better. The officers would then have indulged in a more colorful uniform, especially for the ball given on the anniversary of the victory.

[6] This costume could have had many variations: a fur cap could be worn instead of the tuque, the mitasses might be red or white. Each of the three districts had its own distinctive color; in Three Rivers it was white and in Montreal blue.

Private   Private, Winter Dress   Officer

The Quebec Militia, 1775-1776

His Majesty's Newfoundland Regiment of Foot (Pringle's), 1780-1783

The first permanent settlers came to Newfoundland in the early 17th century and there, as elsewhere in North America, the French and English fought each other to gain control of the island and its fisheries. The Treaty of Utrecht in 1713 gave Newfoundland to Great Britain, and relative peace came to the island until 1762 when a French expedition captured St. John's, its capital. A hasty concentration of British troops made the French position untenable and the force quickly surrendered. However, Newfoundland's defenses were still quite negligible in 1778 when France allied herself with the new United States and declared war on Great Britain. In May 1780, alarming news reached St. John's concerning a possible attack. This was confirmed in September when an American ship, the *Mercury*, was captured with secret dispatches containing proposals for a French invasion of Newfoundland.

On September 20, 1780, Governor Richard Edwards authorized the levy of a regular regiment of 300 men divided into six companies and commanded by Major Robert Pringle. Its mission was to assist the few regulars then in Newfoundland. This garrison was made up of small detachments from the Royal Artillery and the 42nd, 71st, and 84th Regiments of Foot. By the end of November four companies had been raised and the regiment took up its duties while the remaining two companies were being completed. During March 1781 the government in England advised Governor Edwards that the regiment would have only three companies of 100 men each in order to reduce the number of officers which was considered excessive.[1] The *Army List* of 1782 showed one major commanding, two captains, one captain-lieutenant, five lieutenants, three ensigns, one adjutant and a surgeon as the regimental strength.[2]

As events turned out, the French did not attack, and the Regiment garrisoned St. John's until it was disbanded on October 5, 1783.[3] Although it had a quiet existence, the unit had certain peculiarities. It was the first regular regiment of Newfoundlanders to be raised. Instead of the usual red coat, the uniform was a blue coat with red lapels and cuffs (and presumably a red collar), white lining, white metal buttons, white laced buttonholes set in pairs, white waistcoat and breeches, and a hat with a white worsted lace border. Drummers wore a red coat "ornamented with the usual lace on the Seams and Sleeves."[4] The drums were probably blue with red hoops and bearing the cypher and crown in white.

Officers would have worn the same uniform but of better quality. Officers buttons now in the Newfoundland Naval and Military Museum are made of silver and bear a small crown in the center surrounded by decorative devices. The enlisted men's buttons were made of pewter with a larger crown as decoration. On July 20, 1782, this uniform was approved officially with the reservation that the buttons were to be made of plain white metal with the word "Newfoundland."[5] These latter buttons, apparently, were never used.

The figures in this plate wear the uniform described above, fashioned according to the Warrant of 1768.[6] The officer wears a crimson sash, a silver epaulette, a silver-hilted sword to which is attached a gold and crimson sword knot, and a silver gorget engraved with the Royal Arms. The drummer has a white drum belt, a short brass-hilted sword with a curved blade, and a black bearskin cap with a plate having white metal devices on a black ground. The private wears "Long Trousers or Breeches," first worn in January 1782 to replace the "Regimental Breeches," which were mostly worn out.[7] He pays the "complement of the hat" to the officer.

Eric I. Manders
Réne Chartrand

[1]Great Britain, Public Records Office, Colonial Office 194, Vol. 35 (henceforth CO 194/35), folios 71, 82, 88, 100. Microfilm copy at the Public Archives of Canada. G. W. L. Nicholson, *The Fighting Newfoundlander*, Government of Newfoundland, 1964. pp. 17-18.

[2]This is the *Army List* printed in Dublin in 1782. The one printed in London mentions the regiment only the next year.

[3]CO 194/35, folio 222.

[4]*Ibid.* folio 94.

[5]Great Britain, Public Records Office, War Office 30, Vol. 13a, folio 43.

[6]This Warrant of December 19, 1768 is in War Office 30, Vol. 13, and has been published in Charles M. Lefferts. *Uniforms of the American, British, French, and German Armies in the War of the American Revolution*, New York, 1926 (republished in 1971), and Cecil C. P. Lawson. *A History of the Uniforms of the British Army*. London: 1961, Vol. III.

[7]Nicholson, *Ibid.* p. 591 (from extracts of the regimental order book which are reproduced in appendix).

Officer's Button   *Men's Button*

His Majesty's Newfoundland Regiment of Foot (Pringle's), 1780-1783

Anhalt-Zerbst Infantry Regiment, 1778-1783

One of the six German rulers who concluded subsidy treaties with Great Britain to provide soldiers during the Revolutionary War was Frederick-Augustus, Prince of Anhalt-Zerbst. This absentee ruler who did not set foot in his principality from 1773 until his death in 1793, in October 1777 agreed to furnish the British with a regiment of two battalions of 550 men each.

This force could not be recruited from his own principality, which was located about twenty miles southeast of Magdeburg, north of the River Elbe, and numbered approximately twenty thousand inhabitants. Prince Frederick-Augustus, therefore, had to go outside his own dominions for both officers and men.

After much trouble a force of 828 men was finally assembled in the principality. Then, the refusal of Frederick the Great of Prussia to allow the passage of the Anhalt-Zerbst troops through his territory raised new difficulties. Frederick's refusal was not based on any love for the new United States. Instead, faced by the possibility of war with Austria and Russia over the partition of Poland, he wanted to keep all available manpower in Germany. To reach the port of embarkation at Stade, northwest of Hamburg, it became necessary to route the troops through seven different states and free cities. Great difficulties were experienced with deserters and with Prussian recruiting officers, who saw a chance to pick up men easily. Regular skirmishes with these recruiting officers resulted. Of the 828 men who had left the principality, 334 deserted before reaching Stade, and it was only because the colonel in charge of the party was able to enlist about 130 additional recruits en route that the unit was finally able to sail on April 22, 1778, with 625 men.

The transports made a quick passage and arrived before Quebec towards the last of May, but the tribulations of the Anhalt-Zerbst contingent were not over. The British commander at Quebec had not been notified of the arrival of these troops and they were forced to remain aboard the transports in the St. Lawrence River. Upon receipt of instructions from England some three months later the Regiment was finally allowed to land. This contingent, plus two small groups of reinforcements which arrived in 1779 and 1780, thereafter performed garrison duties in Canada until the close of hostilities.[1]

The remainder of the Anhalt-Zerbst Regiment furnished under the subsidy treaty was sent to New York in 1781. This unit, commanded by a major, consisted of 474 souls, including twenty-one women and twelve children. They disembarked on August 14, 1781. The detachment's uniforms, like those of the other German troops, were considered by a contemporary to be too heavy for the hot season then in full swing.

This uniform, however, unlike those of the other German contingents which followed the Prussian in style, was modeled instead after the Austrian. The clothing of the men who landed in New York has been described as follows:

> The Anhalt-Zerbst troops look more like dragoons than Infantry. They are clothed in white, faced with red; Felt caps, a la Hussar; Boots and a red cloak. Their arms are a musket and a bayonet, and a short Sword. Over their waist-belts, which are buckled over their coats, they wear a kind of sash of red and yellow worsted. They are good looking, well sized young men.[2]

Some further details of the uniforms worn in America can be gathered from an original drawing which was at one time in the collection of that great uniform collector, Landgraf Ludwig IX of Hesse Darmstadt. According to this, the red facings were composed of lapels, cuffs, and shoulderstraps; the buttons of the coat were yellow and the coat lining was red; the waistcoat was red with white buttons and a white lining; the belt was red. In addition to this uniform the troops were also furnished with long, linen overalls and linen waist-coats.[3]

Of the approximately 1200 Anhalt-Zerbst troops sent to the scene of the war in America, 984 returned to Germany in the summer of 1783, a remarkably small loss in comparison with that of some of the other German contingents.[4]

Herbert Knötel
Detmar H. Finke

[1]Edward J. Lowell. *The Hessians and the Other German Auxiliaries of Great Britain in the Revolutionary War.* New York: Harper, 1884. pp. 12-13; Charles M. Lefferts. *Uniforms of the American, British, French, and German Armies in the War of the American Revolution, 1775-1783.* New York: New York Historical Society, 1926. pp. 268-269.

[2]Frederick Mackenzie. *Diary . . . as an Officer of the Regiment of Royal Welch Fusiliers, 1775-1781.* Cambridge: Harvard Univ. Press, 1930. entries for August 11, 14 and 15, 1781.

[3]*Buchsweiler Inventar des Landgrafen Ludwig IX von Hessen-Darmstadt.* Inventar No. 1066.

[4]Lowell, *Ibid.* p. 300.

Grenadier, 1778

*Musketeer in
Field Uniform, 1778*

*Musketeer
New York, 1781*

Anhalt-Zerbst Infantry Regiment, 1778-1783

Brunswick Infantry Regiment von Rhetz, 1776-1777

The Regiment von Rhetz was part of the contingent the British government obtained from the Duke of Brunswick in 1776 for service in North America. "The Brunswickers were reviewed and mustered into English service by Colonel William Faucitt, the British Commissioner and plenipotentiary, who was not pleased with the appearance of the soldiers. Many were too old, many were half-grown boys. The uniforms of one group were so bad that the English government was obliged to advance 5000 pounds to re-outfit the men in Portsmouth."[1] The Brunswickers were cheated by English contractors for, when they opened cases of shoes at sea, they found ladies' slippers! No overcoats had been provided, although the troops were destined for a winter campaign in Canada.

Disembarking near Quebec on September 27, the Regiment was involved in General Guy Carleton's abortive autumn invasion of New York, but saw no action. There were some losses from sunstroke, exhaustion, and the general effects of hard marching after the interlude of foul water and worse food aboard the transports. Officers complained that the Regimental colors were a nuisance in the thick timber. The Regiment spent the winter in quarters at Fort Saint Anne. In October, its muster roll showed:[2]

1 Lieutenant Colonel	1 Surgeon Major
1 Major	5 Company Surgeons
5 Captains	1 Clerk
5 1st Lieutenants	1 Drum Major
5 2nd Lieutenants	4 Buglers (Musicians)
5 Ensigns	50 Sergeants and Corporals
1 Adjutant	15 Drummers
1 Quartermaster	41 Officers' valets
1 Chaplain	529 Soldiers
1 Paymaster	

At this time, in keeping with standard Prussian and British practice, the regimental grenadier company was detached to Lieutenant Colonel Breyman's command, the "German Reserve" of grenadiers and light infantry.[3]

Taking part in Burgoyne's expedition with the Specht and Riedesel Regiments the following year, the Regiment formed the 1st German Brigade of the army's left wing. Before departing Canada, the Regiment left behind small details and some sick and disabled. Burgoyne's campaign proved disastrous and, after a series of defeats and with only five days' provisions remaining, the army surrendered at Saratoga on October 17, 1777. The Regiment von Rhetz essentially ceased to exist as a combat unit.

In 1778 the debris from Burgoyne's German regiments plus some replacements received from Europe were reformed into two regiments, Ehrenbrook's and Barner's. The Rhetz survivors were absorbed into Ehrenbrook's unit and finished the war on garrison duty around Trois Rivieres.[4]

The field officer and the ensign in this illustration were taken from original watercolors by Herbert Knötel, the musketeer from a sketch by Harry Larter. The uniforms are typical of the period when most of the minor German states patterned their armies after the Prussian. The Regiment von Rhetz had a medium blue coat with red lining and turnbacks; white collar, lapels, and cuffs; and yellow buttons. Vests and breeches, or overalls, were white although field officers might wear black breeches on compaign. Officers wore gold buttons and lace. Their sashes and sword knots, like those of all Brunswick officers, were mixed white and yellow. The color combinations of officers' sashes often was the quickest means of distinguishing the troops of various minor German states. Officers also wore yellow-metal gorgets bearing the white horse of Brunswick beneath a red-and-white crown all upon a red field. Enlisted men's hats had an edging of white lace; musketeers' sword knots were white with a red top to their tassels. Scabbards were brown; haversacks white; canteens gray; and knapsacks of brown cowhide with brown straps. Pompons varied according to the wearer's grade and company.

The Regimental standard had a light-blue field (some accounts indicate a greenish tinge) divided into four cantons by a white Maltese cross. The Brunswick white horse emblem was in the center on a circular red field surmounted by a red-and-white crown touched with gold. Each arm of the Maltese cross contained a gold grenade; the outer corner of each canton, a gold wreath and a crown. The pike head was yellow; and the cravatte and its tassels, the Brunswick white-and-yellow. In bad weather the standard could be encased in the protective cover the ensign wears over his left shoulder.

Frederick E. Ray, Jr.
John R. Elting

[1]Edward J. Lowell. *The Hessians and the Other German Auxiliaries of Great Britain in the Revolutionary War.* Port Washington, N.Y.: Kennikat Pr., 1965. p. 119.

[2]Great Britain War Office. WO17/1570, p. 139.

[3]George F. Stanley, ed. *For Want of a Horse.* Sackville, N. B.: Tribune Pr., 1961. p. 99.

[4]Material furnished by Major Charles Stewart, Librarian, Canadian Department of National Defence.

Ensign with Regimental Standard   *Private*   *Field Officer
Campaign Dress*

Brunswick Infantry Regiment von Rhetz, 1776-1777

Brunswick Regiment of Dragoons, 1776-1783

Colonel William Faucitt, the British officer charged with the purchase of German mercenaries, professed himself pleased with one of his acquisitions, the Brunswick Regiment of Dragoons. Not one of the men was drunk as he embarked them on March 13, 1776, for transport to North America!

The Dragoons formed a part of the Brunswick contingent under Major General Baron Friedrich von Riedesel — "Red Hazel" to the irreverent British private. Despite their cavalry uniforms and equipment, they were taken into British service as infantry, "His Majesty of Great Britain" agreeing to provide horses if future developments demanded they be mounted.

On arrival in Quebec, the Regiment appears to have numbered some 336, all ranks.[1] It moved south with Burgoyne in 1777, still on foot, about 227 strong. On August 16, Lieutenant Colonel Friedrich Baum with some 150 of his dragoons, forming the backbone of a mixed detachment sent out to gather horses and supplies, were overrun near Bennington by American forces under John Stark. The remainder of the Regiment were at Saratoga. Horses had been found for about thirty men and these were used to patrol the rear of the British army for a brief time after the battle of Freeman's Farm.

During the period of captivity after the surrender at Saratoga, efforts were made to enlist many of the Brunswickers in the American army, particularly by Lieutenant Colonel Charles Armand who was recruiting energetically for his "legion." Some Brunswickers joined the legion; many of them deserted back to the British as soon as possible.

Despite all disaster, the Regiment, again stationed in Canada, had a strength of 282 men in 1779; this included men left in Canada in 1777, new replacements, and exchanged or escaped prisoners. A detachment of exchanged prisoners was formed on Long Island where Riedesel commanded after being exchanged.[2]

Generally speaking, the uniform of this Regiment is well known. However, this plate illustrates several unusual features. One major source of disagreement has been the blue-and-white striped trousers shown on the dragoon in field uniform. Riedesel states flatly that he secured these for all the Brunswick troops, beginning with the dragoons and his own regiment of infantry. Old "Red Hazel" was considered a reliable officer; his account should be accurate. Furthermore, some watercolors — apparently done by a contemporary amateur artist — inserted into a copy of Riedesel's *Memoirs* in the New York Public Library show Brunswick infantry in such clothing.[3] It is probable that these trousers were used for marching, drill, and fatigue. The regular dragoon uniform would have been worn for ceremonies. From all accounts, none of

which are too clear, it would appear that the dragoons marched to Bennington in leather breeches and boots. This, however, would have been natural since they hoped to secure mounts there.

By custom in the various German principalities during this period, only infantry officers wore the gorget. Possibly the Brunswick Dragoons officers adopted it because they were serving as dismounted troops.

The drummer's uniform is taken from a water color by the late Herbert Knötel. Whether or not all the drummers were negroes in 1776 is not certain. Black musicians were fashionable, and many German regiments used them. An account of the Regiment after its return to Germany notes that "Among them were some black men enlisted by General Riedesel as drummers."[4] The drummer wears a silver dog collar; this appears to have been a widespread military custom.

One uncertain feature of this plate is the guidon carried by the underofficer. Apparently the regimental colors were left in Brunswick, only four small blue guidons being brought to America. These were described as blue, ornamented in gold; one side carried the Brunswick coat of arms and the other, a white horse on a green field against a red background as shown in the plate. The spearhead is copied from that of a Brunswick infantry regiment; the staff, from an original in the West Point Museum. The shape and size of the guidon are based upon a contemporary Prussian dragoon guidon. These guidons apparently were hidden from the Americans after Saratoga. Stories vary as to detail, but it appears that Riedesel ordered the staffs of all the Brunswick flags to be burned, and the colors themselves sewed into a mattress. He reported to General Horatio Gates that the colors had been burned with the staffs. Later, the mattress was smuggled through the American lines into New York.

After the Revolution, the Regiment returned to Brunswick. Its beloved Duke, however, specifed that only able-bodied native Brunswickers with good service records were wanted; the remainder could stay in America!

Frederick T. Chapman
John R. Elting

[1] Ray W. Pettengill, tr. *Letters from America, 1776-1779.* Boston: Houghton Mifflin, 1924. p. XIX.

[2] Carl L. Baurmeister. *Revolution in America, Confidential Letters and Journals, 1776-1784.* Translated by B. A. Uhlendorf. New Brunswick, N.J.: Rutgers Univ. Press, 1957. p. 429.

[3] Max von Eelking. *Memoirs, and letters and Journals, of Major General Riedesel, during his Residence in America.* Albany: J. Munsell, 1868. p. 101.

[4] Joseph G. Rosengarten. *American History from German Archives.* Lancaster, Pa.: The Pennsylvania-German Society, 1904. p. 35.

Non-Commissioned Officer   Drummer   Officer   Dragoon in service uniform

Brunswick Regiment of Dragoons, 1776-1783

Hesse-Cassel Artillery, 1776-1782

Among the contingent of Hesse-Cassel troops that came to America during the Revolutionary War were three field companies of Artillery commanded by Lieutenant Colonel Hans Heinrich von Eitel, contracted for by Great Britain in the treaty signed January 15, 1776 with Frederick II, Landgrave of Hesse-Cassel. These three companies represented the entire Artillery Corps of Hesse-Cassel. In fact, two of the companies had to be newly raised and trained in order to meet the terms of the treaty.[1] As with the Hessian infantry, effort was made to adjust tactics and organization to the British systems and, while waiting arrival of transports from January to March 1776, the artillerymen drilled with their guns in Cassel.

Each artillery company consisted of five officers and one non-combatant, fourteen non-commissioned officers, three drummers, and 129 men.[2] Their guns initially were light four-pounders although other calibers certainly were used later.

When the first Hessian division sailed from Bremen on April 17, 1776, there was room for only 242 officers and men of the artillery. This detachment landed on Staten Island on August 15, and a week later crossed the Narrows to take part in the battle of Long Island. This was their first fight. Thereafter, some element of the Hesse-Cassel Artillery took part in almost every battle, serving with different German corps or with the Royal Artillery.

Although the Hessian artillery uniform, dark blue with red facings, somewhat resembled that of the American Continental gunners, there were many minor differences. The Hessian red was more crimson; their coats were without collars; and their waistcoats and trousers were yellow instead of white. It is interesting to note that there was an overall similarity between the artillery of all the armies in the Revolution — all wore dark blue coats with red facings, yellow buttons, and black felt hats. This similarity was more than a coincidence for the relationships between artillerists of different countries was close and sympathetic. There was a constant exchange of scientific data and drill manuals between the various states.

The left figure in this plate shows the sergeant in command of the gun section. His grade is indicated by the wide lace on his cuffs and his cane. A short linstock with its smoldering length of slow match is thrust into the ground on his right. The private in the foreground holds a fuzed shell. He is equipped with the short saber and musket which were the artilleryman's personal weapons. The wide white-leather belt over his left shoulder supports a large, round artillery flask. A gunner's vent pick is attached to the front of his belt. The private to his left holds a small priming flask and wears a shoulder belt of heavy webbing. This belt, termed a "bricole", and its attached rope were used when the gun crew dragged and manhandled their gun into position. The rather primitive horse harness of the period and the fact that artillery drivers were hired civilians usually prevented the use of horses under fire. The soldier seated on the gun trail also carries a large artillery powder flask. The private on the extreme right wears a bricole and holds a rammer-staff. Note the long queues, a peculiarity of German troops.

Herbert Knötel
Frederick P. Todd

[1]Claus von Bredow. *Historische Rang-und Stammliste des Deutschen Heeres.* Berlin: 1905. pp. 616-617.

[2]Joseph G. Rosengarten. *The German Allied Troops in the North American War of Independence, 1776-1783.* Albany: J. Munsell, 1893. p. 22; Edward J. Lowell. *The Hessians and the Other German Auxiliaries of Great Britain in the Revolutionary War.* New York: Harper, 1884. *Passim.* The non-combatant probably was a "company surgeon."

Hesse-Cassel Artillery, 1776-1782

Hesse-Cassel Field Jaeger Corps, 1776-1783

The treaty between King George III and the Landgrave of Hesse-Cassel for German troops to serve in America provided two companies of Field Jaegers. These light troops had first been raised in Hesse-Cassel in 1758 and had taken part in the Seven Years' War with France. They were trained marksmen recruited from among hunters and gamekeepers.[1]

The need for men skilled in woods fighting had been foreseen as early as 1776, and that need grew as the American Revolution continued. Subsequent agreements were reached for more Hessian Jaeger companies. By the summer of 1777, there were five foot companies with an authorized strength of 1067 officers and men, nominally formed into the Field Jaeger Corps under Lieutenant Colonel Ludwig Johann Adam von Wurmb. Actually, the Corps totalled scarcely 500 men and officers, and it is quite certain that it never reached its full strength. Because detachments were always being drawn off for special missions, the Corps is credited with an impressive number of American battle honors including Flatbush, White Plains, Trenton, Brandywine, and Yorktown.

The Hesse-Cassel Jaegers wore green coats with crimson collars, lapels, cuffs, and linings and green waistcoats. Mounted Jaegers wore leather breeches; those of the foot Jaegers were green to match their coats. Either white or buff breeches were worn during hot weather. During their American service, the foot Jaegers replaced their boots with high gaiters of brown leather or cloth. Their equipment was of buff leather. Jaegers wore green cockades and on parade wore tall plumes in their cocked hats. The color of these plumes varied based upon the Jaeger's grade and, possibly, his company.

This green and red uniform was typical of similar units in all German armies. European huntsmen and foresters had favored green clothing since the early Middle Ages and this color became a symbol of their trade. When the Prussian Army formed its first regular Jaeger unit in 1744, it was given a green uniform with red facings to emphasize its military status.[2] The smaller German states dutifully followed suit with minor modifications. The Brunswick and Anspach-Bayreuth Jaeger companies, which also served with the British, differed little in appearance from the Hesse-Cassel Corps.

The Jaeger's weapon was a short, heavy rifle, somewhat larger in caliber than the average American rifle. Weapons varied greatly since many were the individual Jaeger's personal property. Most were plain and rather massive firearms with simple brass mountings and patch boxes with sliding wooden covers in the butt. The Jaeger rifle was the direct ancestor of the American rifle, many of which resembled it. It was equal to the American in accuracy except at extreme range. Like American riflemen, the Jaeger used a "patched ball" and could load and fire as rapidly as his opponent.[3] Neither the American or Jaeger rifle were made to take bayonets. The foot Jaeger therefore carried a straight two-edged "hunting" sword approximately twenty-two inches long. As is shown in this plate, the scabbard for this sword often had a built-in sheath on its outer surface for a hunting knife. Mounted Jaegers carried light cavalry sabers and pistols although they normally fought dismounted.

Though handicapped by the problems of obtaining qualified replacements, the Jaegers were probably the most effective of British mercenaries, and were used as skirmishers, scouts, and snipers. They used hunting horns for signalling. Proud of their elite status thoroughly disciplined, and led by veteran officers, the Jaegers worked efficiently with line infantry, a technique the individualistic American rifleman learned the hard way.[4]

Herbert Knötel
Frederick P. Todd
John R. Elting

[1]Claus von Bredow. *Historische Rang-und Stammliste des Deutchen Heeres.* Berlin: 1905. pp. 609-610; Edward J. Lowell. *The Hessians and Other German Auxiliaries of Great Britain in the Revolutionary War.* New York: Harper, 1884. pp. 20, 107-108. "Jaeger" can be roughly translated as "Hunter;" a "feldjaeger," therefore, was a hunter in military service.

[2]Prussian War Office: *Geschichte der Bekleidung, Bewaffnung und Ausrustung des koniglich preuszischen Heeres.* Weimar: 1902. Vol. III, pp. 60 ff.

[3]Harold L. Peterson. *Arms and Armor in Colonial America, 1526-1783.* Harrisburg: Stackpole, 1956. As a very rough approximation, a typical jaeger rifle was forty-five inches in length and was caliber seventy.

[4]Samuel S. Smith. *Fight for the Delaware, 1777.* Monmouth Beach, N. J.: Peter Freneau, 1970. p. 18.

Mounted Jaeger   *Foot Jaeger*

Hesse-Cassel Field Jaeger Corps, 1776-1783

Hesse-Cassel Fusilier Regiment von Ditfurth, 1776-1782

The von Ditfurth Regiment was raised in 1702, and from 1765 to 1782 it was designated as a fusilier regiment.[1] At this period, in the Prussian system which dominated most German armies, there was no difference between the fusilier and the musketeer regiments in tactical employment nor was there any difference in armament although they wore different types of headdress. Not until later did the fusilier become a form of light infantry, halfway between the musketeer and the jaeger.

By the treaty signed by the Landgrave of Hesse-Cassel with the British government on January 15, 1776, the Regiment von Ditfurth was destined for service in North America. Colonel William Faucitt, British emissary, stated that ". . . The Regiments Garde du Corps, Prince Carl, General Ditfurth, General Trumbach are likewise outstanding and suitable for any type of service. It is difficult to state which of them is the best. . ."[2]

Commanded by Colonel Carl von Bose, the Regiment sailed with the first contingent of Hessians in March of that year. After a long and arduous voyage marked with illness caused by spoiled stores and bad water, the Regiment landed at Staten Island on August 15. For a short time, it was an element of the 2nd Hessian Brigade under Major General Johann von Stirn and took part in the battle of Long Island and, possibly, the storming of Fort Washington.

The Regiment's grenadier company had been assigned to the 3rd Grenadier Battalion commanded by Lieutenant Colonel von Minnergode, together with the grenadier companies from three other regiments. This was common practice in both the various German and the British armies of the time. By chance, von Minnergode's battalion was also a part of von Stirn's brigade.

In November 1776, the Regiment was sent to Newport, Rhode Island, where it remained on peaceful garrison duty except for a few weeks of alarm during the abortive French and American attack in August 1778. Lieutenant Frederick MacKenzie, 23rd Regiment of Foot (Royal Welch Fusiliers), in his diary entry for January 28, 1778, compared the Hessian regiments with his own insofar as the health of their men was concerned:

> Notwithstanding the frequent changes in the weather, the healthiness of this Island is beyond a doubt. As proof of it, the three Hessian Regiments of Ditfurth, Huyne, & Bunau, amounting to nearly 1800 effective men, have not more than 70 Sick men on the lists, of all descriptions. The Landgrave's Regiment, indeed, out of 560 men, have about 60 Sick . . . The Sick of the British Regiments have in general been more numerous than the Hessians. During the last Campaign, we never had less than 100, sometimes 180 Sick, out of 1700 men.[3]

MacKenzie attributed part of the illness in the Hessian regiments to the lack of clothing and shoes among the enlisted ranks. He notes on March 24, 1778, that ". . . The Hessian Regiments stationed on this Island, put on their new Clothing this day for the first time. Altho it has been ready for three months past, they could not put on until they received order to do so from General Knyphausen, their Commander-in-Chief in America. These troops have received no clothing since they left Germany in the beginning of the year 1776."[4]

In October of 1779, the Regiment returned briefly to New York, and there embarked for South Carolina. After a stormy voyage, it arrived in February, 1780, under the command of Colonel Max von Westerhagen. It participated in the seige of Charleston and spent the remainder of its American service in that southern city. Charleston was evacuated in December 1782, and the Regiment von Ditfurth sailed for home shortly thereafter.

The uniforms shown in this plate remained almost unchanged throughout the life of the Regiment. Its facings were always yellow, although at an earlier date its buttonholes had been edged with white. In 1782, the battalion companies exchanged their fusilier caps for cocked hats bound with white lace.

Herbert Knötel

[1] Charles M. Lefferts. *Uniforms of the American, British, French, and German Armies in the War of the American Revolution, 1775-1783.* New York: New York Historical Society, 1926. pp. 263-265, refers to this unit inadvisedly as a musketeer regiment and, relying too heavily on British returns, misspells its name. Herr Knötel has made use of official drawings in the Grand Ducal Library in Darmstadt for his information on uniforms and equipment.

[2] Ernest Kipping. *The Troops of Hesse-Kassel in the American War for Independence, 1776-1783.* Typescript translation by Thurman E. Philoon, 1973, in the MS Collection, U.S. Army Military History Research Collection, Carlisle Barracks, Pa.

[3] *Diary of Frederick MacKenzie.* Cambridge: Harvard Univ. Press, 1930. p. 239.

[4] *Ibid.* p. 259.

Field Officer   *Fusilier*   *Grenadier*

Hesse-Cassel Fusilier Regiment von Ditfurth, 1776-1782

Hesse-Cassel Fusilier Regiment Erbprinz, 1780

The use of mercenary soldiers was not rare in 18th century warfare nor was it unusual for the Landgraves of Hesse-Cassel to provide troops to other nations. As early as 1687, over a thousand soldiers from Hesse-Cassel served under Venetians fighting the Turks. In 1702, 9000 Hessians served the maritime powers; in 1706, 11500 were in Italy. England, however, was the best customer of the Landgraves for she had Hessians in her pay for a large part of the 18th century.[1] The treaty of January 15, 1776 between the two nations provided for fifteen regiments of Hesse-Cassel troops serving in North America. The treaty did specify, in addition to the payments to be made to the Landgrave, that the troops were to be kept together under their own general and that the sick were to be cared for by their own surgeons. Supplies and equipment were to be provided by the British.[2]

The Hesse-Cassel Fusilier Regiment Erbprinz was an old Regiment, formed in 1680. Its elevation to fusilier status, however, dated only from 1775, such "elevation" consisting of little more than a change of headgear from the three-cornered hat to the fusilier cap. Tracing the service of various German units during the American Revolution is a complicated task. Many of them were identified only by the names of their commanding officers. Commanders changed frequently and their names were often misspelled, Anglicized, or Gallicized. "Erbprinz" frequently appears as "Prince Hereditaire," "Hereditary Prince," or "Crown Prince." It is also occasionally confused with the Hesse-Hanau Regiment Erbprinz which served with Burgoyne.

The Fusilier Regiment von Erbprinz was among the first units mustered at Bremelehe in March 1776. British emissary, Colonel William Faucitt, stated that, "... Five other corps were mustered for this day: a grenadier battalion, Colonel Block, the fusilier regiments Erbprinz, Knyphausen, Murbach, and Donop. All five are unusually handsome regiments completely uniformed and fit for any service in the whole world ... "[3] The Regiment arrived in America with the first contingent of German troops on August 12, 1776, and was subsequently involved in the fighting around New York. It remained in the New York area until 1781 when it was sent to Virginia to join Cornwallis' command. It was part of the forces surrendered by Cornwallis at Yorktown.

Although the Regiment had an authorized strength of 660 men and officers, its actual strength appears to have been considerably less. At the surrender at Yorktown, however, only 484 were included on the Regimental rolls. Landers cites the Regiment's losses during the Yorktown campaign as twenty-three killed, fifty-seven wounded, and sixteen missing.[4]

In 1780, the Regiment reverted to its original status as a "musketeer" unit. The fusilier hat was replaced by the cocked hat, and the rose-red regimental facings reverted to the "carmoisin-red" worn previous to 1775. This plate shows both uniforms. The officer at left center appears in the uniform worn when the Regiment arrived in New York. Shortly afterward, the Regiment's officers adopted the common practice of the British Army — a practice sparked by American terrain and sharpshooters — and removed the expensive embroidery from their coats. Although the spontoon continued to be carried while in garrison, many of the officers armed themselves with fusils, a practice later widely condemned. Sergeants and corporals, however, retained the "Kurzgewehr" for field service; the corporal in this plate is so armed. The arms used by the Regiment during its American service were the English musket and bayonet, and the Hessian side-arm or cutlass.[5]

After the surrender at Yorktown, the Hessian prisoner-units were marched slowly northward to Frederick, Maryland. Here they remained in prison camps until May 1783 when they were released and marched to New York preliminary to embarking for the long voyage home.

Herbert Knötel
John R. Elting

[1]Edward J. Lowell. *The Hessians and the Other German Auxiliaries of Great Britain in the Revolutionary War.* Port Washington, N. Y.: Kennikat Press. 1965. p. 2.

[2]*Ibid.* pp. 2-3.

[3]Ernest Kipping. *The Troops of Hesse-Kassel in the American War for Independence.* Typescript translation by Thurman E. Philoon, 1973, in MS collection of U.S. Army Military History Research Collection, Carlisle Barracks, Pa., p. 39.

[4]H. L. Landers. *The Virginia Campaign and the Blockade and Siege of Yorktown, 1781.* Washington: U.S.G.P.O., 1931. pp. 213-214.

[5]Charles M. Lefferts. *Uniforms of the American, British, French, and German Armies in the War of the American Revolution, 1775-1783.* New York: New York Historical Society, 1926. p. 258.

Fusilier, 1775   *Officer, 1775*   *Officer, 1780*   *Corporal, 1780*

Hesse-Cassel Fusilier Regiment Erbprinz, 1780

Commander-in-Chief's Guard, 1777-1783

The Commander-in-Chief's Guard, often called "The Life Guard," was formed by General Orders dated March 12, 1776.[1] During most of its service, the Guard was a company-size infantry organization composed of carefully selected men. From time to time, however, details from the four Continental Light Dragoon Regiments were attached to it. Between May 1777 and September 1778, these details were provided largely by George Baylor's 3rd Regiment of Continental Light Dragoons.[2] Later, detachments were drawn from the regiments of colonels Theodoric Bland, Elisha Sheldon, and Stephen Moylan. The Provost Troops of Light Dragoons also normally was attached to the Army headquarters.

It was the duty of the infantry of the Guard to guard the headquarters and to insure the safe-keeping of the papers and effects of the Commander-in-Chief as well as the safety of his person. The attached dragoons accompanied him on marches and reconnaissance. They were also used as couriers and served as patrols and videttes. Both dragoons and infantry were used in battle when the occasion demanded.

The Guard initially numbered approximately fifty men. At Valley Forge, Major General von Steuben increased the Guard to about 150 men, including two drummers, and used the group as a demonstration company. For much of its remaining service, the Guard included some seventy men and officers. After July 1782, the unit included a small fife and drum corps and a drum major. Men selected for the Guard were native-born Americans, five feet nine inches to five feet ten inches tall. During 1777-1778, its men appear to have been primarily Virginians. After 1778, however, men were selected from throughout the Army. The Guard's commander, Captain Caleb Gibbs, was a "Yankee."

With the war almost over, the Guard was disbanded and its men discharged on June 6, 1783. The headquarters at Newburgh, New York, thereafter were guarded by details provided by New England regiments stationed at that post. The last service provided by this provisional guard was the delivery of Washington's personal papers to Mount Vernon in November 1783.

The lack of definite information concerning uniforms so common to all Continental units also applies to the uniform of the Guard. This is undoubtedly due to the recurrring clothing shortages and to the compromises which had to be made. The first significant reference to clothing of the Guard is a description of a deserter in the *New York Gazette* of June 17, 1776. This described the uniform as being a blue coat faced with buff and a red waistcoat. It should be noted, however, that the deserter also had " . . . a blue coat faced with green and a round unbound felt hat."[3]

George Washington Parke Custis described the dress of the Guard as " . . . a blue coat, with white facings; white wasitcoat and breeches; black stock and black half gaiters, and a round hat, with blue and white feathers."[4] Although he refers to no particular date, this actually would appear to be the uniform of the men detailed to form the provisional guard at Newburgh in 1783.

The description accompanying the 1784 drawing of an officer of Washington's "Independent Company," by Daniel N. Chodowiecki and the drawing itself show the uniform as light blue faced with a "reddish yellow buckskin."[5] This is the only known contemporary picture of a Guardsman and one cannot be entirely confident of its details.

Washington in a letter to Captain Gibbs in April 1777 vaguely substantiates the blue coat faced with buff. An item from Elijah Fisher's journal suggests the men wore caps in 1778.[6] Andrew D. Mellick described the Guard uniform (probably on the authority of the *New York Gazette* item quoted above) as: " . . . blue coat, faced with buff, red waistcoat, buckskin breeches, white body belts, and a black felt cocked hat bound with white tape."[7] The uniforms shown in the plate are based upon the references cited above and represent at least one phase of the Guard's history. The cocked hat probably preceded the bearskin crested cap, but both could have been worn simultaneously.

H. Charles McBarron, Jr.
Frederick P. Todd

[1] Carlos E. Godfrey. *The Commander-in-Chief's Guard.* Washington, D. C.: Stevenson-Smith, 1904.

[2] *Ibid.* pp. 36-40.

[3] Charles M. Lefferts. *Uniforms of the American, British, French, and German Armies in the War of the American Revolution, 1775-1783.* New York: New York Historical Society, 1926. p. 86.

[4] *Recollections and Private Memoirs of Washington,* New York, 1860. pp. 256-257.

[5] Daniel N. Chodowiecki. *Allgemeines Historisches Taschenbuch . . .* Berlin; 1784. Reproduced in *Military Collector & Historian.* Vol. VI, December 1954. p. 91.

[6] Gibbs commanded the Guard during 1776-1783, the letter is quoted in Godfrey, *Ibid.* pp. 40-41. "Elijah Fisher's Journal" is in the *Magazine of History,* Extra Number 6 (1909).

[7] *The Story of an Old Farm,* Somerville, N. J.: 1889. p. 478.

Commander-in-Chief's Guard, 1777-1783

Continental Infantry, 1778-1783

In August 1782, Major General Nathanael Greene, watching beside the deathbed of British rule in the Southern Colonies, once more spoke his mind on the neglect his command was suffering. Beef, when it was available, was "perfect carrion" — but even worse was the state of half his troops, "entirely naked, with nothing but a breech cloth about them and never came out of their tents, and the rest were ragged as wolves." A subordinate added the final grievance, "We have not had a drop of Spirits in Camp for more than a month."[1]

This was one of the last choruses of a continual theme song of suffering which underlay the Revolution. As the American Army filed into its winter camp at Valley Forge, Brigadier General Anthony Wayne had written, "Not one Whole Shirt to a Brigade. For God's Sake if you can't give us anything else — give us linen that we may be Enabled to Rescue the poor Worthy fellows from the Vermin which are now Devouring them . . . Some hundreds we thought prudent to Deposit some six feet under Ground who have Died of a Disorder produced by want of Clothing." Officers were "Covered with Rags and Crawling with Vermin."[2] A French officer notes, "I saw officers, at a grand parade — mounting guard in a sort of dressing gown, made of an old blanket or woolen bed cover."[3] Prisoners and deserters from Washington's forces were described as "almost naked and generally without shoes — an old, dirty blanket around them attached by a leather belt around the waist."[4] Inspector General Baron von Steuben noted that the cartridge boxes were in bad shape and short supply, pieced out with powder horns and tin boxes.

The same story was told by Major General John Sullivan in 1777: "the whole without watch coats, one half of them without blankets and more than one third without shoes and stockings and breeches and many without shirts. Indeed the officers in sundry cases are destitute of proper clothing, some being almost naked", and, again in 1779, on his return from the Iroquois country: "I have neither shoes, shirts, Blankets, hats, stockings, nor leggings to relieve their necessities."[5] Even the elegant Wayne found himself compelled to try to make three short coats out of three old battered long ones, and spend his own money to clothe his men.

These miseries had many sources. During the worst of Valley Forge, the patriotic merchants of Boston would not sell any of their plentiful supply of clothing to the Army except at a profit of 1000 to 1800 percent, cash on the barrel head.[6] Once secured, stocks of clothing were likely to be lost, mislaid, or stolen. Poor roads, incompetent quartermasters, and a shortage of transport all hampered supply. "Some thousands of sutes of clothing complete has been set to Peeks Kill. There many lay-a rotten when so many brave men are Fresing. Ware is the fault."[7] Connecticut troops at Valley Forge were well uniformed, as were the Pennsylvanians in 1779, while soldiers from other states went half naked. Both states, however, refused to share their surplus.

There was also lack of common sense in the issue of available clothing. As Colonel William Davis wrote Governor Thomas Jefferson of Virginia on January 25, 1781, reporting another American column reduced to breechclouts and odd blankets, " . . . a mistaken system has too long prevailed in the mode of clothing our men. Saving and preserving are almost as important as supplying in the first instance. A coat properly patched is nearly as useful as a new one. Yet we have nothing given us for the necessary purpose of repairing — instead of mending old clothes we are always asking for new. A good pair of stockings is given to a naked soldier today; he has no shoes and wears them out by the next week and in a fortnight when the stockings are gone he got his shoes. Or perhaps he got breeches but no lining to them, a new coat or fashionable hat but no shirt — or if he has he is without breeches . . ."[8]

Finally, soldiers were frequently careless of their new uniforms: "the Rogues and whores that went with the baggage" might pilfer it; or the soldier trade articles of it for drink. But beyond all this, America was a rough place for campaigning. Cloth and shoes wore out faster than in Europe. Englishman and German mercenary, too, often went ragged.

The Continentals shown here may have been well clothed — or even smartly uniformed — when the current campaign began. Now, they have only fragments of patched clothing. The officer in the foreground wears "country boots", pieces of cloth folded around the leg and tied at knee and ankle, much like Indian leggings.

Nevertheless, these are fighting men — by now tough, professional soldiers. They need no breeches to beat the British.

H. Charles McBarron, Jr.
John R. Elting

[1] John C. Miller. *Triumph of Freedom*. Boston: Little, Brown, 1948. p. 678.

[2] *Ibid*. p. 221.

[3] Charlemagne Tower. *The Marquis de La Fayette in the American Revolution*. Philadelphia: Lippincott, 1926. Vol. I, p. 323.

[4] John F. Watson. *Annals of Philadelphia and Pennsylvania, in the Olden Time*. Pennsylvania: the author, 1845. Vol. II, p. 287.

[5] *Journals of the Sullivan Expedition*. Frederick Cook, New York: 1887. p. 308.

[6] Miller. *Ibid*. p. 223.

[7] *Revolutionary Letters to Col. Pickering*, Vol. 43M, Essex Inst. Hist. Collect., Salem: 1908. p. 7.

[8] *Virginia State Papers*, Vol. I, Richmond: p. 462.

Continental Infantry, 1778-1783

14th Continental Regiment (Glover's Marblehead Regiment), 1775-1776

On January 10, 1775, over three months before the fight at Concord, a town meeting was held in Marblehead, Massachusetts, "...to make provisions to pay persons who may enlist as minute men, and to take other suitable steps for perfecting the militia in the arts of war."[1] Out of this meeting came a provisional regiment of minute men detached from the militia of Essex County, the ancient East Regiment formed in 1636. On May 14, the new unit was formally organized as the Marblehead (or Marine) Regiment, Massachusetts Provincial Army, with John Glover as its colonel. It transferred to the Continental Army about two months later and on January 1, 1776, was redesignated the 14th Continental Regiment.

Colonel Glover was a prominent ship owner of Marblehead and before the war had been engaged extensively in the fishing trade. His regiment was recruited from the hardy class of men he was accustomed to employ. "His command was always efficient, and had more than the usual discipline. Colonel Glover was small in stature, and as Major-General the Chevalier de Chastellux writes, was 'an active and a good soldier.' "[2]

The Massachusetts Provincial Congress resolved on July 5, 1775 to furnish its regiments with 13000 coats, adding:

> ...That each coat must be faced with the same kind of cloth of which it is made; that the coats be made in the common, plain way, without lappels, short and with small folds.[3]

It is not certain that the Marblehead Regiment received an issue of these coats, but if it did, the cloth was drab or brown in color and lapels of red were added. Descriptions of the Regiment's uniform in 1776 and 1777 speak of a "...light colored coat with red lappels, buckskin breeches, blue stockings," and a "...brown regimental coat faced with red, a felt hat."[4]

Many of the Marblehead men retained items of clothing they had worn as fishermen and sailors. One man had a "white cap, frock, and trousers"; another, a "blue coat with leather buttons, tarred trousers."[5] Using contemporary cartoons and paintings of American seamen, these salty costumes have been reconstructed for this plate. The men are shown with British infantry muskets. The captain wears the single epaulet on the right shoulder prescribed by the British

service and later adopted for Continental regulations.

The Marblehead Regiment took no active part in the siege of Boston, but remained on the seacoast in the vicinity of Beverly, Massachusetts, until it was directed to march to New York on July 20, 1776. Although stationed on the mainland of New York during the battle of Long Island, the Regiment did man the boats which evacuated Washington's forces from Long Island the night of August 29-30. The Regiment also manned boats used to move heavy bagaage out of New York City on September 13.

Meanwhile, Colonel Glover had been placed temporarily in command of a brigade on September 4. Active fighting for the Regiment then began with a vengeance. On October 18, Glover's brigade, consisting of the 14th and three other Massachusetts regiments, fought an expert delaying action at Pell's Point, New York. The brigade was a part of Washington's battered main army in its retreat across New Jersey and participated in the victorious counteroffensive at Trenton and Princeton. Perhaps the greatest moment for the Regiment occurred on Christmas Eve, 1776, when it manned the boats which ferried the Americans across the ice-clogged Delaware River to surprise the Hessians at Trenton.

The 14th Continental Regiment was discharged in January 1777 when the enlistment terms of its men expired. Its major, William R. Lee, was promoted to colonel and authorized to raise Lee's Additional Continental Regiment. Some of the original Marbleheaders apparently reenlisted in this unit.[6]

H. Charles McBarron, Jr.
Frederick P. Todd

[1] Frank A. Gardner. *Glover's Marblehead Regiment in the War of the Revolution.* Salem, Mass.: Salem Press, 1908. *passim.*
[2] William S. Stryker. *The Battles of Trenton and Princeton.* Boston: Houghton, Mifflin, 1898. p. 346.
[3] *American Archives,* 4th set., Vol. II, p. 1486.
[4] Charles M. Lefferts. *Uniforms of the American, British, French, and German Armies in the War of the American Revolution, 1775-1783.* New York: New York Historical Society, 1926. pp. 75, 79.
[5] *Ibid.*
[6] The "additional" Continental regiments were authorized by a panicked Continental Congress, December 1776, in addition to the established state quotas. Most of the regiments failed to secure sufficient recruits.

Captain   *Privates*

14th Continental Regiment (Glover's Marblehead Regiment), 1775-1776

Webb's Additional Regiment, Continental Line, 1777-1781

Except for the blue and buff of Washington and his staff, no uniform of the American Revolution has more interest and romance attached to it than the scarlet dress of Webb's Regiment. There were other redcoated units on the American side of the struggle, but these soldiers from Connecticut made the most of their unusual attire.

Samuel Blatchey Webb was active in Revolutionary affairs at an early age. He marched to Boston in 1775 as a lieutenant of a light infantry company of the 2d Connecticut Regiment and rapidly rose to lieutenant colonel and aide-de-camp to Washington. He was wounded at Bunker Hill, White Plains and Trenton. While recuperating from the last wound, he was commissioned colonel and authorized to raise one of the sixteen Additional Continental Regiments. He returned to Connecticut early in February 1777 to do this.[1]

In November of the year before, Captain John Paul Jones with the *Alfred*, in company with Captain Hoysteed Hacker on the *Providence*, were cruising off the Canadian coast when they captured a large armed ship named the *Mellish*. Investigation proved she carried a rich cargo of military clothing going out to the British regiments in Canada. So valuable was the cargo that Jones kept her under convoy. He wrote to the Marine Committee later: "This prize is, I believe, the most valuable that has been taken by the American arms ... The loss will distress the enemy more than can be easily imagined, as the clothing on board of her is the last intended to be sent out for Canada this season, and all that has preceded it is already taken." These were uniforms made for either the 9th, 20th, 29th or 34th Regiments of Foot, then in Canada. The *Mellish*, under a prize crew, ran through Nantucket shoals and reached Boston in mid-December. There she was unloaded by John Bradford, the Continental Agent.[2]

Word of the capture reached Webb before he had left the main army in New Jersey, and he secured Washington's reluctant permission to uniform his regiment in red. He took north with him this authority, signed by the Continental Quartermaster-General, Thomas Mifflin:

> Colonel Webb has his Excellency's, General Washington's orders to appropriate so much of the scarlet clothing taken from the Enemy at Sea, as will be sufficient to cloath one Regiment. The said clothing to be set apart for his Regt.[3]

Armed with this document he seems literally to have seized the captured uniforms as they passed through Connecticut, much to the concern of Governor Trumbull. When, probably with his own funds, he procured 500 additional hunting shirts, waistcoats and overalls, Trumbull told Washington about it and the General wrote Webb a stinging letter of rebuke:

> ... What is the meaning of all this? ... Can you conceive it necessary that your Regiment is to have one Suit for parade and another to march to New Haven? Present appearance render it doubtful whether they will ever get further, or intend to leave the State of Connecticut. ...
>
> I well remember that you, to obviate My objections to Cloathing your men in red, propos'd Hunting shirts as a covering; but I then observed that this could not be expected at the Public expense, nor had I any conception that you could have entertain'd the most distant thought of drawing these things from the Public Stores, where you must have known how difficult a matter it is to provide for the large demands of the Army ...[4]

Webb's reply has not been found, but it must have satisfied Washington, for no further action was taken. The regiment continued to wear scarlet. The journal of one of his officers tells of buying a "Scarlet Coat" at Wethersfield in December 1777.[5] Deserter descriptions mention: "Scarlet regimental coat faced with yellow, light colored waistcoat and breeches" (November 1778); "Regimentals: scarlet faced with yellow, white vest and breeches" (February-March 1799); and "Red uniform coat faced with yellow" (February 1780).[6]

Possibly because of its smart uniforms, Webb's regiment had an excellent record for discipline and combat efficiency. In July 1780 it was redesignated the 9th Connecticut Regiment.

The company officer on the left carries a fusil, or light musket. As late as 1777 this practice appears to have been common, but thereafter the espontoon gradually took the place of the fusil until all company officers were required by general orders to carry them.

H. Charles McBarron, Jr.
Frederick P. Todd

[1] *Dictionary of American Biography*; Worthington C. Ford, ed. *Correspondence and Journals of Samuel Blackley Webb*. New York: Wickersham Press, 1893.

[2] Gardner W. Allen. *A Naval History of the American Revolution*. Boston: Houghton Mifflin, 1913. Vol. I, pp. 122, 127; *American Archives*, 5th Series, Vol. III, *passim*; George F. Emmons. *The Navy of the United States, from the Commencement, 1775 to 1853.* Washington: Gideon, 1853. pp. 42-43.

[3] Ford. *Ibid.* pp. 214-216.

[4] John C. Fitzpatrick, ed. *The Writings of George Washington*. Washington: U.S.G.P.O. 1931-44. Vol. VII, p. 229 and Vol. VIII, pp. 196-197. Ford. *Ibid.* Vol. I, pp. 214-237; Trumbull's letters to Washington about the matter can be found in Washington Papers, MSS Division, Library of Congress.

[5] "Deacon Nathan Beer's Journal." MSS Division, Library of Congress.

[6] Charles M. Lefferts. *Uniforms of the American, British, French, and German Armies in the War of the American Revolution, 1775-1783.* New York: New York Historical Society, 1926. p. 81.

Officer and Privates of a Battalion Company

Webb's Additional Regiment, Continental Line, 1777-1781

Colonel John Haslet's Delaware Regiment, Continental Line, 1776

This famous regiment was created when Congress on December 9, 1775, authorized the lower Counties of Delaware to raise a battalion (regiment) of eight companies. The Delaware Committee of Safety acted immediately and organized the Regiment to serve until December 31, 1776 " . . . unless sooner discharged" and submitted the name of John Haslet as colonel. Staff and company officers were commissioned and the roster of officers was complete by January 21, 1776.[1]

Haslet, then colonel of the Lower Regiment, Kent County Militia, had served in the 1758 expedition against Fort Duquesne as a captain in Colonel James Burd's 2nd Pennsylvania Regiment.[2] Lieutenant Thomas Holland, a former British army officer, was appointed adjutant. These two officers were responsible for infusing spirit and discipline into the new Regiment.[3]

Officially mustered on April 12, the Regiment totalled 726 officers and men.[4] By May they were completely uniformed and equipped in a manner suggesting a deliberate intention of forming a superior unit patterned after the elite British light infantry. Line officers were armed with fusils, and short coats and caps provided for all ranks. Congress appropriated $38,500 of the then undepreciated currency for the Regiment's support.[5] It has been stated authoritatively that this was the best uniformed and equipped regiment in the army in 1776.[6]

The uniforms shown in this plate were reconstructed from many sources, but especially from two unpublished water colors by Charles M. Lefferts, accompanied by detailed descriptions thereon, and the official Delaware State painting of the Regiment by Stanley M. Arthurs.[7] The coats were dark "Dutch" blue faced and lined with scarlet; the waistcoats, white flannel. White cotton breeches and wool stockings with black linen spatterdashes completed the uniform. Buttons were pewter, stamped with initials "DB." The small round caps of black jacked leather had a high peak in front inscribed in gilt with "Liberty and Independence — Delaware Regiment" with a sheaf of wheat in the center scroll, and surmounted by the Delaware crest of a full-rigged ship. When paraded, all ranks wore a short red plume on the left side of the cap and their hair was dressed with powder. Haversacks were made of white canvas and cross belts of white buff leather supported the bayonet scabbard and the black leather cartridge box. A brown-painted canvas knapsack, a wood canteen, and a blanket completed the field equipment.[8]

Serious threat of a major Tory uprising kept the Regiment on duty in Delaware until July 20 when, ordered to Philadelphia, they marched north from Dover in full regimentals and field kit. Their smart appearance attracted much comment.[9] On August 7, Congress directed that the Regiment be completely rearmed with new imported English bayonets and muskets " . . . as good guns as you could wish to see."[10] In their letters after the battle of Long Island, Hessian officers praised the courage, appearance, and fine arms of the Delaware troops, describing them as "the Regiment Stirling in their blue and Red coats."[11]

In September, Congress voted to raise a new Continental Army with Delaware's quota again being one battalion. Troops were to enlist for three years or the duration of the war. Haslet accepted a new commission as colonel on December 5, 1776, and was joined by ten of his former officers and many of their men. Most of the men were paid, discharged, and sent home to recruit the new regiment.[12] The old Regiment, then consisting of eight officers and 92 men, fought its last battle as a unit at Trenton.[13] Haslet was killed at Princeton on January 3, 1777.

H. Charles McBarron, Jr.
James P. Simpson

[1]*Delaware Archives.* 1911. Vol. I, pp. 34-35.

[2]Christofer L. Ward. *The Delaware Continentals.* Wilmington: Historical Society of Delaware, 1941. p. 539.

[3]*Ibid.* pp. 6, 517-520; Enoch Anderson. "Personel Recollections." *Historical Society of Delaware Papers.* Vol. XVI, p. 7-8.

[4]*Delaware Archives.* Vol. I, pp. 39-61.

[5]Ward. *Ibid.* p. 8.

[6]Charles M. Lefferts. *Uniforms of the American, British, French, and German Armies in the War of the American Revolution, 1775-1783.* New York: New York Historical Society, 1926. pp. 26-27, plate VII.

[7]Stanley Arthurs. *The American Historical Scene.* Philadelphia: Univ. of Pennsylvania Press, 1935. pp. 46-47.

[8]Lefferts, *Ibid.* p. 26, and detailed descriptions on two unpublished water colors made for S. M. Arthurs in 1914.

[9]Anderson, *Ibid.* pp. 16-20; John T. Scharf. *History of Delaware, 1609-1888.* Philadelphia: L. J. Richards, 1888. p. 236.

[10]Caesar Rodney. *Letters to and From Caesar Rodney, 1756-1784.* Philadelphia: Univ. of Pennsylvania Press, 1933. p. 102; Anderson, *Ibid.* p. 20.

[11]Thomas W. Feld. "The Battle of Long Island." *Long Island Historical Memoirs,* Vol. XI, 1869. pp. 391-438.

[12]Rodney, *Ibid.* p. 146.

[13]Ward, *Ibid.* p. 137.

Private   *Captain*   *Private*

Colonel John Haslet's Delaware Regiment, Continental Line (Delaware Blues), 1776

Colonel David Hall's Delaware Regiment, Continental Line, 1777-1783

Although a nucleus of veterans from John Haslet's Delaware Regiment reenlisted, a number of factors — including the death of their Colonel at Princeton — discouraged recruiting for the new Delaware Continental formation. By January 31, 1777, only two of the eight companies proposed were considered sufficiently complete for service.[1] The Delaware Assembly ordered these troops to Philadelphia where they were completely uniformed, equipped, and armed, joining the army at Princeton on March 27.[2]

Their new regimentals, supplied by the army's Clothier General, included some changes from their previous uniform. Coats were still dark blue with red facings, cuffs, and turnbacks, but of longer cut. Waistcoats were white; more durable buckskins replaced the white cotton breeches; and they now wore cocked hats trimmed with yellow braid.[3] Arms and accouterments were unchanged except that new field equipment issued later included tomahawks (camp hatchets) and a black japanned metal cannister to hold forty extra cartridges.[4] Subsequently authorized were watch coats for officers, swords and belts for first sergeants, and espontoons for company officers.[5]

Incentive for service was stimulated by Congressional bounties of land and money, supplemented by a Delaware annual bounty of clothing. This bounty promised every man "1 Regimental coat, 1 jacket without sleeves, 1 pair Buckskin breeches or 2 pair Woolen or Linnen Ditto, 1 Hat or Leather Cap, 2 Shirts, 1 Hunting Shirt, 2 pair Overalls, 2 pair Stockings, 2 pair Shoes, and 1 Blanket."[6]

The remaining six companies and three new field officers — Colonel David Hall, Lieutenant Colonel Charles Pope, and Major David Vaughn (all three promoted from captain) — arrived at Princeton on May 19. The Regiment now totaled 312 officers and men and was again assigned to Smallwood's Maryland brigade.[7]

The "New Establishment" ordered by Congress on May 22, 1778, added a ninth company to the Regiment; and Captain John Patten's company was designated as light infantry.[8] Inspection reports of this company indicate that both cocked hats and the Delaware's original caps were worn. During this same period, records of Delaware's Clothier General report that material for breeches was becoming scarce and that increased quantities of "tow linnen overalls" were sent to the troops.[9]

A lottery conducted for distribution of new uniforms of various colors received from France in October 1779 gave the Delaware Regiment blue coats with red facings. These were the last full regimentals issued until 1783.[10]

Ordered to join the Southern Army, the Regiment marched from Morristown on April 17, 1780, to win enduring fame by their desperate heroism at Camden. After that disaster, survivors were reorganized as two companies of light infantry under Captain Robert Kirkwood and established a reputation as the elite of the Southern Army.

In October 1780, North Carolina, from its meager stores, furnished each of these men with new shoes, a hunting shirt, and blue-striped ticking overalls. This was the uniform worn at their subsequent actions at Cowpens, Guilford Court House, Hobkirk's Hill, the siege of Ninety-Six, and Eutaw Springs.

A part of 85 recruits, sent from Delaware in August 1781 to reinforce Kirkwood, was diverted to Yorktown where they served with artillery units until Cornwallis's surrender. These troops, "dressed in hunting shirts and ragged overalls; then continued south to join the Delaware battalion whose muster rolls showed 168 men in all ranks by May 21, 1792."[11]

Sent home in November, the Delaware troops arrived at Christiana Bridge, Delaware, on January 17, 1783.[12] New clothing, arms, and equipment were issued. On March 11, the War Office ordered the battalion increased to four companies and 56 recruits were added for this purpose. The men trained until officially disbanded in October 1783.

H. Charles McBarron, Jr.
James P. Simpson

[1]*Delaware Archives.* Vol. I, pp. 85, 543.

[2]Robert Kirkwood. "Journal and Order Book," *Historical Society of Delaware, Papers.* Vol. LVI, 1910. p. 50.

[3]Charles M. Lefferts. *Uniforms of the American, British, French, and German Armies in the War of the American Revolution, 1775-1783.* New York: New York Historical Society, 1926. pp. 98-99; Enoch Anderson. "Personal Recollections." *Historical Society of Delaware Papers.* Vol. XVI. pp. 29,52.

[4]Kirkwood, *Ibid.* pp. 177-182, 195, 205-206.

[5]*Delaware Archives.* Vol. I, pp. 591-593, Vol. II, p. 1040.

[6]*Delaware Archives.* Vol. I, pp. 543, 585.

[7]*Delaware Archives.* Vol. I, (Payrolls 1777); Christofer L. Ward. *The Delaware Continentals.* Wilmington: Historical Society of Delaware, 1941. p. 170.

[8]*Delaware Archives.* Vol. I, p. 142; Ward, *Ibid.* pp. 286-287.

[9]*Delaware Archives.* Vol. I, pp. 190-191; Vol. II p. 1036.

[10]Ward. *Ibid.* p. 319.

[11]Major Caleb P. Bennett, "The Delaware Regiment in the Revolution," *Pennsylvania Historical Society,* 1881. p. 459.

[12]Bennett, *Ibid.* p. 42; Kirkwood, *Ibid.* p. 30; Ward, *Ibid.* p. 482.

Private
1781

Private
1778

1778

Private, Light Company
1778

Captain

Colonel David Hall's Delaware Regiment, Continental Line, 1777-1783

Light Infantry Company, 4th Massachusetts Regiment, Continental Line, 1781-1782

It is unusual that the best description of the uniform of the Light Infantry Company of the 4th Massachusetts during the period it garrisoned the Hudson Valley and fought at Yorktown is provided with a woman who served with the unit! Posing as a man, Deborah Sampson of Plympton, Massachusetts, joined the Regiment at West Point and was assigned to Captain George Webb's Light Infantry Company. Although there are questions as to the exact period of her enlistment and although one may wonder at the patriotic innocence of her exploit, there is no doubt that she did serve with this Company in 1782.

The light infantry — one picked company in each Continental infantry regiment — were the elite of the United States Army. (Deborah must have been a tall, strapping lass!) On campaign, they normally were detached from their parent regiments for special missions and were regrouped into provisional light infantry battalions after the British custom. Brigadier General Anthony Wayne led this "Corps of Light Infantry" to capture Stony Point in 1777. In 1781, as the "Light Division", it served under Major General de Lafayette in Virginia.

The clothing and equipment issued Deborah is described by her biographer as

> ... a French fusee, a knapsack, cartridge-box, and thirty cartridges ... Her garb was exchanged for a uniform peculiar to the infantry. It consisted of a blue coat lined with white, with white wings on the shoulders and cords on the arms and pockets; a white wasistcoat, breeches or overhauls and stockings, with black straps about the knees; half boots, a black velvet stock, and a cap, with variegated cockade, on one side, a plume tipped with red on the other, and a white sash about the crown. Her martial apparatus, exclusive of those in marches, were a gun and bayonet, a cartridge-box and hanger with white belts.[1]

This uniform was in general that prescribed by George Washington for the New England Line on October 2, 1779. It was set forth in instructions issued by the Massachusetts Bay government in January 1781 since Massachusetts at that time was responsible for clothing and equipping its units serving with the Continental Line.[2] The "cords" or braiding, a non-regulation item, as shown in this plate are based upon the contemporary French uniform style. "Wings" — traditionally the mark of an elite unit — are of the type shown in the sketch of a light infantry officer of the 2nd Massachusetts Regiment drawn by Colonel Thaddeus Dosciuszko.[3] The three soldiers shown in the plate wear "overalls", long trousers cut snug to the leg and shaped to fit over the top of the shoe like a gaiter. Properly fitted, overalls provided freedom of action and more protection than the knee breeches and stockings worn earlier in the war. The drummer wears the regulation "reversed colors", a white coat with blue facings. A number of such drummers' coats were included in a shipment of blue-and-white uniforms sent from France to Virginia in 1782.[4]

The light infantry caps shown are modeled on those worn by four light infantry officers on the far right side of John Trumbull's first painting of the British surrender at Yorktown.[5] Deborah's "variegated cockade" was the "Union Cockade" worn by American troops of this period which combined the United States black cockade with the French white. The tall black-and-red plumes are probably those brought from France by Lafayette for wear by the light infantry. A French officer noted these at Yorktown, flaunted above rags and bare feet.[6]

The company officer in the plate is distinguised by his silver epaulette and crimson sash. He is armed with an espontoon and a hanger. The latter was a short cutting sword. Its issue to enlisted men at this time seems unusual based upon present knowledge. However, the hanger was carried by elite chasseur and grenadier companies of the French infantry and may have been adopted by American light infantry units as another symbol of their similar status.

The 4th Massachusetts Regiment, originally Colonel Ebenezer Learned's Massachusetts Battalion, was one of twelve such units formed by the state on May 19, 1775. The Regiment entered Continental Service on June 15 to serve until December 31, 1775. The Regiment was mustered out on January 2, 1776. Learned at once reorgainzed the unit as the 3rd Continental Regiment. On January 1, 1777, the Regiment was again reorganized and redesignated the 4th Massachusetts; as such it fought under William Shepard through 1782. In January 1783, Colonel Henry Jackson assumed command; the Regiment was disbanded on November 3. Jackson formed the 1st American Regiment — the last infantry unit of the Continental Line — the same day. Seventeen of his officers and many men of the 4th went with him.[7]

H. Charles McBarron, Jr.
Frederick P. Todd
John R. Elting

[1]John A. Vinton. *The Female Review: Life of Deborah Sampson ...* Boston: 1866. pp. 133, 134.

[2]Henry Whiting. *Revolutionary Orders of General Washington.* New York: Wiley and Putnam, 1844. p. 164; Detmar H. Finke and H. Charles McBarron, Jr. "Continental Army Uniforms and Specifications, 1779-1781." *Military Collector & Historian.* Vol. XIV, Summer 1962. pp. 35-41.

[3]Miecislaus Haiman. *Kosciuszko in the American Revolution.* New York: Polish Institute of Arts and Sciences in America, 1943. p. 336.

[4]*Calendar of Virginia State Papers.* Vol. III, p. 336.

[5]Now in the Yale School of Fine Arts, New Haven.

[6]John Elting. "A Comment on Yorktown." *Military Collector & Historian.* Vol. XXV, Winter 1973. p. 200.

[7]This unit, which was disbanded June 20, 1784, should not be confused with the second First American Regiment, authorized by Congress June 3, 1784 and now the 3rd Infantry Regiment.

Musician   Private   Company Officer

Light Infantry Company, 4th Massachusetts Regiment, Continental Line, 1781-1782

5th Pennsylvania Regiment, Continental Line, 1777-1783

The 5th Pennsylvania Regiment was created on January 1, 1777, around the old 4th Pennsylvania Battalion. Colonel Anthony Wayne, who had commanded the 4th, assumed command of the new regiment. Shortly, however, he was promoted and his old school friend, Colonel Francis Johnson, took it over.

Recruited largely from Chester County, the Regiment was one of the two units that did not immediately join the famous mutiny of the Pennsylvania Line in 1781. According to the diary of Captain Joseph McClellan of the 9th Pennsylvania Regiment "the 9th and 5th Regiments were kept in their parades until they were threatened by the others, if they did not move off they would turn the artillery on them, several shots being fired over their heads."[1] Bowing to such good arguments, the two regiments then joined the mutiny.

The Regiment began the war in full uniform, the blue coats with white facings selected for the 4th Battalion being carried over into the new organization. The greatest number of deserter descriptions mention a dark-blue uniform coat, faced with white; buckskin breeches; an unflapped hat; and blue year stockings.[2] A few hunting shirts were always present, but these were not issued to the Regiment in large quantity. For example, on November 30, 1777, the Regiment issued 560 regimental coats, but no hunting shirts.[3] By February 1778, however, the supply of white cloth suitable for facings had run out in Pennsylvania, and red apparently was supplied in its place.[4]

The button indicated is a flat pewter button originally issued to the 4th Battalion.[5] The only Pennsylvania buttons so far discovered are for the 1776 battalions, and all deserter descriptions indicate that they were in use throughout the war and were not replaced by regimental buttons.

As the war progressed, Pennsylvania found it more difficult to uniform its Line. "I believe no Army before this was ever put to such shifts in order to have even the appearance of uniformity," wrote Brigadier General Anthony Wayne to President Reed of Pennsylvania.[6] An example of the appearance of the Pennsylvania Line at this point can be taken from Thompson Westcott's deserter descriptions for early 1779: "Gen. Wayne's division: Blue regimental coats, lined with white; ruffled shirts; red flannel leggings; and a sort of cap dressed up with fur."[7]

By 1781, regimental coats were no longer being issued; blue cloth was not "procurable at any Rate of Price."[8] Wayne reported to Reed that he was having his men make short coats out of "old, tattered long ones."[9] Hunting shirts replaced coats throughout the Pennsylvania Line. Colonel Thomas Craig, commanding a Pennsylvania brigade, reported his men "were marched away in a linen Hunting Shirt, Overalls and Vest of the same."[10]

Those enlisted men who still wore regimental coats generally had the old ones with white facings, while many of their officers had procured blue regimental coats faced with red, as prescribed in the general orders of 1779. This greatly concerned General George Washington who wished to make the best and most military impression on the French. He instructed General Wayne to have the necessary red material to replace the men's facings sent from Pennsylvania. General Wayne forwarded the request to President Reed, adding that he thought the changes would take four days. Another problem in making the Regiment look military lay with the men's hats. "I thought on an expedient," reported Wayne, "of reducing the heterogenous of old, new, cock'd & floped hats & pieces of hats, to Infantry Caps, in which we succeeded very well — by making three decent caps out of one tolerable & two very ordinary hats, to which we added by way of embellishment, a white plume and a Comb of red hair."[11]

H. Charles McBarron, Jr.
Philip R. N. Katcher

[1]Joseph McClellan. "A Diary of the Revolt" in: John B. Linn and William M. Engle. *Pennsylvania in the War of the Revolution*. Harrisburg: L. S. Hart, 1880. Vol. II, p. 631.

[2]Peter F. Copeland. "Clothing of the 4th Pennsylvania Battalion, 1776-1777." *Military Collector & Historian*. Vol. XVIII. Fall 1966. pp. 69-74.

[3]Samuel Hazard. *The Pennsylvania Archives*. Harrisburg: 1853. Vol. VI. p. 46.

[4]*Ibid.* p. 285.

[5]William Calver and Reginald Bolton. *History Written with Pick and Shovel*. New York: New York Historical Society, 1950. p. 92.

[6]Hazard. *Ibid.* Vol. VIII. p. 593.

[7]John R. Elting. "The Thompson Westcott Descriptions of Military Dress During the American Revolution." *Military Collector & Historian*. Vol. XII. Spring 1960. pp. 1-5.

[8]Hazard. *Ibid.* Vol. IX. p. 373.

[9]*Ibid.* Vol. VIII. p. 593.

[10]*Ibid.* Vol. IX. p. 600.

[11]*Ibid.* Vol. VIII. pp. 451, 593.

Private, 1778

Sergeant, 1777   Lieutenant Colonel, 1777   Private, 1778   Private, 1781   Lieutenant, 1779

5th Pennsylvania Regiment, Continental Line, 1777-1783

13th Pennsylvania Regiment, Continental Line (The Pennsylvania Regiment), 1776-1778

After the first draft of Pennsylvania troops had been raised in the Fall of 1775 and early 1776 and had joined the main Continental Army, it was evident that troops were still needed in Pennsylvania. Therefore, on February 20, 1776, two battalions were authorized, one of riflemen and one of "musketmen." Drawn mainly from the Lancaster area, the riflemen were placed under the command of Colonel Samuel Miles and the musketeers under Colonel Samuel J. Atlee. The men, who were to serve until January 1, 1778, received a bounty of shoes, stockings, and hats. They were to bring their own arms.[1] In April 1777, having joined the Continental Army and been much reduced in numbers at the battle of Long Island, the two battalions were combined and designated the Pennsylvania State Regiment.[2] The following November, Congress accepted the Regiment for Continental Service as the 13th Pennsylvania Regiment under the command of Colonel Walter Stewart.

The hunting shirt was apparently the most common uniform in the rifle battalion. Richard Barnit and Daniel Graham of Captain John Murray's company wore "light-colored fringed hunting shirts and trowsers" when they were captured after deserting.[3] John Fitzgerald, a deserter from Captain Andrew Long's company, wore a "black hunting shirt and trowsers."[4]

The musketry battalion was more traditionally uniformed. Adam McElroy and several others of Captain Joseph McClellen's company wore blue coats faced with red, white stockings and waistcoats, buckskin breeches, and regimental hats bound up yellow.[5]

This blue and red uniform, similar to that worn by some German units, several times led to trouble for the Regiment. On October 23, 1776, the unit while on a scouting party ran into the Delaware Battalion which also wore similar uniforms. In the words of one of the Pennsylvanians, ". . . taking the Delaware Blues for the enemy, we fired on each other, in which six of our riflemen and nine of the Blues were killed."[6] Earlier, on the retreat from Long Island, the Battalion came too close to a German unit which they thought to be Continentals, probably because of similarly colored uniforms.

Red facings, however, were not the only ones in the Regiment. Colonel Stewart requested ". . . trimming of 300 suits of cloathes, which I would to be blue and red if possible, as I know White cannot now be obtained."[7] There is one deserter description which reports a blue coat with white facings. Despite the non-uniformity of uniforms, there was a regimental button.[8]

Regardless of how the Regiment was supposed to be clothed or what color its facings were supposed to be, raggedness was the real order of the day. On August 2, 1776, Atlee wrote that his " . . . battalion is without either shirts, breeches, or Stockings."[9] After the Long Island fiasco, one lieutenant wrote: "I wish you would endeavor to send me such of my clothes as are worth wearing . . . there are no clothes to be got here of any kind. I have lost all my shirts and stockings except two shirts and two pair of stockings."[10]

The situation improved little as the Regiment became more settled. Toward the end of the Regiment's service, Colonel Stewart again wrote the President of Pennsylvania saying, "My hopes of getting the Regiment genteelly and well cloathed this campaigne are vanished unless your Excellency and the Council will assist me in it."[11]

On July 1, 1778, the Regiment was combined with the 2nd Pennsylvania Regiment under the latter's number, and Colonel Stewart assumed command of the combined unit.

P. R. N. Katcher
Dennis Martin

[1]John B. Linn and William M. Engle. *Pennsylvania in the War of the Revolution.* Harrisburg: L. S. Hart, 1880. Vol. I, p. 193.
[2]*Ibid.* p. 257.
[3]*Ibid.* p. 218.
[4]*Ibid.* p. 207.
[5]*Pennsylvania Gazette*, Philadelphia, Pa., July 24, 1776.
[6]This story and an excellent day-by-day account of the Regiment's movements from recruiting to the encampment at Valley Forge appears in James McMichael, "Diary of the Pennsylvania Line, 1776-1778," in *Pennsylvania Magazine of History*, Vol. XVI, pp. 129-159.
[7]Samuel Hazard, *Pennsylvania Archives.* Philadelphia, 1883. Vol. VI, p. 285.
[8]William Calver and Reginald Bolton. *History Written with Pick and Shovel.* New York: New York Historical Society, 1950. p. 139.
[9]Hazard. *Ibid.* Vol. V, p. 6.
[10]Linn and Engle. *Ibid.* Vol. I, p. 196.
[11]Hazard. *Ibid.* p. 258.

Sergeant

Rifleman   *Musketman*

dennis martin

13th Pennsylvania Regiment, Continental Line (The Pennsylvania Regiment), 1776-1778

2nd Virginia Regiment, Continental Line, 1775-1778

Originally raised for one year's state service, the 2nd Virginia was accepted by Congress for Continental service in March 1776.[1] While assisting in the campaign around Norfolk, the 2nd wore the dress which Virginia's Convention of Delegates authorized for regular troops: hunting shirts with cape and cuffs, leggings, and round hats. The Regiment was equipped with muskets, bayonets, cartouche boxes or pouches, and canteens.[2] The records of the Virginia Public Store confirm the execution of the Convention's intention adding that blue leggings were universally adopted. A deserter from Captain Francis Taylor's Company was reported wearing a trimmed brown hunting shirt and trousers.[3]

Shortly before the Regiment departed in December 1776 to join the main Army under Washington, the Virginia Council of State ordered:

> That a sufficient quantity of blue cloth and trimmings be delivered by the Keeper of the Public Store to Col. Alex. Spottswood Comdr. of the 2nd Regt. in order to equip each Private soldier now . . . enlisted with a short coat . . .[4]

On February 10, 1777, the Continental Board of War ordered the Regiment to Maryland's Eastern Shore to suppress local "insurgents." The Regimental tailors, however, remained in Philadelphia to make up the cloth provided by Virginia.[5] Because of the relatively substantial allotment of uniforms issued, the Regiment continued to wear this uniform until the entire Virginia Line went into red-faced blue uniforms in 1779.

The uniform illustrated in this plate evolved gradually in contrast to the uniform adopted in 1779. For example, when Lieutenants Catesby and Thomas Jones joined the Regiment at Williamsburg in mid-1776, they wore blue uniform coats with bound buttonholes and edging, white waistcoats, blue breeches, and Russian drill spatterdashes which had been made at their father's expense in Northumberland County.[6] In early September 1777, a Colonel Spottswood placed an advertisement for thirteen deserters including a sergeant, a corporal and two privates who carried off their " . . . Regimentals of Blue with white worsted Binding . . . " as well as a private who had a blue hunting shirt.[7] In March 1778, a horse was stolen by one Perry Patterson, who was described as:

> . . . a soldier, a short well set young man of a fair complexion, brown short curled hair, appears to be country born, his clothes regimental, his coat blue, the button holes bound with white, his jacket and breeches white cloth, a mean small brimmed hat.[8]

The only Perry Patterson listed in Gwathemy's authoritative *Historical Record of Virginians in the American Revolution* served with the 2nd. Whether or not he is the same horse thief described in a Pennsylvania newspaper dated in December 1777 as belonging " . . . to the Virginia troops . . . " and wearing a blue regimental coat with white buttonholes is conjectural.[9] In March 1778, a drummer from Captain Jones' Company wearing a blue coat with blue velvet collar, a grey waistcoat, buckskin breeches, and a round hat escaped from the hospital at Euphrata, Pennsylvania.[10]

Timothy Pickering, former Continental Quartermaster General, writing in 1826 to criticize contemporary militia styles, stated: " . . . the best form of [hat] which I ever saw for military men was that adopted by Colonel Spottswood, who commanded a Virginia regiment of continental troops in the campaign in 1777. It was low crowned and the brim was about two and a half or three inches wide, and looped up only on the left side of the head . . . and to that side the cockade was fixed."[11]

Peter F. Copeland
Marko Zlatich
Donald M. Londahl-Smith

[1]*Proceedings of the Convention of Delegates . . . First Session,* July 17-August 26, 1775, Richmond: 1816. p. 29; *Journals of the Continental Congress,* Washington, D. C.: 1906. Vol. V, p. 235.

[2]*Proceedings of the Convention of Delegates . . . Second session . . .* through January 15, 1776, Richmond: 1816. pp. 105-111; *Calendar of Virginia State Papers,* Richmond: 1890. Vol. VIII, p. 123.

[3]Alexander Pardie. *Virginia Gazette,* No. 84, September 6, 1776.

[4]*Journals of the Council of the State of Virginia,* Richmond: 1931. Vol. I, p. 278.

[5]*Papers of the Continental Congress,* Item 147, Vol. I, folio 74, National Archives, Record Group 360.

[6]Papers of the Jones Family of Northumberland County, Virginia, Vol. 20, folio 4591; Vol. 21, folios 4636, 4644, 4702.

[7]Dixon and Hunter. *Virginia Gazette,* No. 1379, September 5, 1777.

[8]Alexander Purdie. *Virginia Gazette,* No. 161, May 1, 1778.

[9]*Pennsylvania Packet or the General Advertiser,* December 17, 1777.

[10]*Ibid.* March 11, 1778.

[11]*American State Papers, Military Affairs,* Washington, 1832, Vol. II, p. 473.

Company Officer   Privates   Drummer

2nd Virginia Regiment, Continental Line, 1775-1778

6th Virginia Regiment, Continental Line, 1776

The extensive use of the "rifle" or "hunting" shirt as a field uniform by American soldiers of the Revolution is well recognized. However, its use during the early years of the war, particularly in Virginia, as a formal uniform with distinctions in color is less understood. A wide variety of colors and types of hunting shirt were used; undoubtedly uniformity would be found only within single companies. Some idea of how these Virginia troops appeared can be gained from the orders issued by the 6th Regiment scarcely a month after it had been organized.[1]

The 6th was one of the first nine battalions or regiments raised by Virginia for the Continental service in February and March 1776, under authority of the act of its Convention of December 1, 1775. With the 1st, 8th, and 9th Battalions, and possibly others, the 6th was encamped at Williamsburg during the spring of that year. Mordecai Buckner was its colonel.

On April 3, it received this order;

> It is recommended to the Colonels to make their men appear as uniform as possible in their Dress, that their Hatts shall be cut, all cocked in Fassion, that their Hair be likewise cut exactly the same length. When the Regiments are under Arms, the Officers to appear in their Hunting shirts; the Officers as well as men to die their shirts in an uniform manner. These attentials may appear Trivial, but they are in fact of considerable importance, as they tend to give what is called Esprit de Corps, without which Regiments never grow to Reputation.[2]

To comply with the order, Colonel Buckner instructed that:

> The Captains of the 6th Battalion, together with the other Officers, are immediately to provide themselves with Hunting Shirts, short and fringed; the men's shirts to be short and plain, the Sergeants' shirts to have a small white Cuffs and plain; the Drummers' shirts to be with dark Cuffs. Both Officers and Soldiers to have Hatts cut round and bound with black; the Brims of their Hatts to be two inches deep and cocked on one side, with a Button and Loop and Cockades, which is to be worn on the left. Neither man nor Officers to do duty in any other Uniform. The Officers and Soldiers are to ware their Hair short and as near a like as possible.[3]

It will be noted that the colors of the hunting shirts are not mentioned. In the month following, a soldier deserted from the Regiment wearing a " . . . hunting shirt dyed black,"[4] but this may not have been an issue garment. Several deserter descriptions made in the summer and fall of 1776 mention hunting shirts " . . . trimmed with red."[5] Gray Virginia broadcloth appears to have been the later uniform of the Regiment. When Lafayette joined the army under Washington in 1777, he remarked that the " . . . best garments were a sort of hunting shirts, loose jackets made of gray linen, very common in Carolina."[6] Gray, therefore, has been used as the basic color of the shirts shown in this plate.

The men wear common overalls, and the officer has buckskin breeches with brown canvas gaiters similar to the type used in the British army for marching. He also sports a buck's tail over his small hat. The muskets are of a kind which might have been issued by the local Committees of Safety although they do not conform to Virginia specifications. One would have been carried by the officer as directed by the Regimental Order issued in May:

> Those Gentlemen officers who has no swords are to procure them immediately, and not to appear on the parade without them, and when their men are going to exercise, the officers are to take their Fuzees in their hand.[7]

The so-called "round hat" worn by the Virginia regiments was preferred to the usual "cocked" or three-cornered hat because it did not collect snow or rain and was lighter and more comfortable, especially in bad weather.

H. Charles McBarron, Jr.
Frederick P. Todd

[1] Charles Campbell, ed. *The Orderly Book of That Portion of the American Army Stationed at or Near Williamsburg, Va., Under the Command of General Andrew Lewis.* Richmond: 1860. pp. 13-14.
[2] *Ibid.*
[3] *Ibid.*
[4] *Virginia Gazette*, May 10, 1776.
[5] *Ibid.* July 5 and November 8, 1776.
[6] Charlemagne Tower. *The Marquis de LaFayette in the American Revolution.* Philadelphia: J. B. Lippencott, 1895. p. 217.
[7] Campbell. *Ibid.* p. 35.

Drummer

Sergeant

Company Officer

6th Virginia Regiment, Continental Line, 1776

Rhode Island Train of Artillery, 1775

The reorganization and expansion of the Rhode Island militia in 1774 included the formation of two new volunteer companies, the Providence Train of Artillery and the Providence Fusiliers. In April 1775, these were combined to form "The United Company of the Train of Artillery of the Town of Providence," thereafter usually termed "The United Train of Artillery." Commanded by Major John Crane, it was assigned to the Rhode Island brigade which Brigadier General Nathanael Greene led to join the American forces besieging Boston.[1]

Its organization at this time was described as:[2]

1 Major and Commandant	2 bombardiers
1 captain	4 gunners
3 lieutenants	4 musicians
2 sergeants	74 matrosses
4 corporals	1 conductor

The musicians were "fifes and drums"; the conductor apparently responsible for the unit's supply, transportation, and maintenance. For armament, the train had four brass field pieces, probably four or six-pounders, and twelve eighteen and twenty four-pounders. The latter seem to have been an assortment of old and dubious weapons of varied origin, but they nevertheless comprised most of the Americans' available siege artillery until Henry Knox brought better guns to Boston from Ticonderoga. The Rhode Island artillerymen naturally could not man all of these guns simultaneously and must have been employed by detachments at the various batteries and on minor operations. On July 8, 1775, for example, Crane with two guns supported a successful attack on a British outpost.[3]

Crane was sometimes referred to as "captain" and the United Train of Artillery as "Crane's Company."[4] During the reorganization of the American army in January 1776, the United Train — or rather those of its men who would re-enlist — were absorbed into Knox's Massachusetts Artillery Regiment (formerly Colonel Richard Gridley's), Crane becoming the latter unit's "first major."[5]

During the battle of Long Island, "a two-gun battery under Captain Benajah Carpenter of Rhode Island" formed part of Lord Stirling's Brigade on the American right flank.[6] They fought their guns gallantly and with fair effect until Stirling was overwhelmed and Carpenter killed.[7] Crane was made colonel of the 3rd Continental Artillery Regiment in June 1776.[8] Since this regiment was recruited chiefly in Massachusetts,

any connection between it and the United Train would appear tenuous. It is noteworthy that the United Train of Artillery was promptly reactivated in 1776 as a Rhode Island militia unit which saw considerable service against British amphibious raids during the remainder of the war.[9]

Like many other American regiments at the beginning of the War, the United Train wore brown coats. Its facings were red; its buttons brass, stamped with Rhode Island's anchor device. Waistcoat and breeches were white linen. Enlisted men wore short black gaiters. Officers wore boots, one or more gold epaulettes according to grade, and the conventional red sashes. The Train's headgear was unique: a cap made of six triangular pieces of jacked leather with a small red-and-brown tuft at the crown. To this was attached a frontal piece whose odd shape may have been inspired by the classic Phrygian or "liberty" cap. Carpenter's cap, later picked up on the Long Island battlefield, is now in the Fraunces Tavern Museum in New York City. It is black with a silver anchor painted on the center of the frontal piece. Above the anchor is a red scroll with "For Our Country" in silver letters. Below the anchor on a gold scroll is the black-lettered motto "In Te Domine Speramus" (In Thee, Lord, Is Our Hope). Other trimming and decoration is in gold. The enlisted men's caps may have been somewhat simpler.

Tom Jones
John R. Elting

[1] J. J. Richards. *Rhode Island's Early Defenders and Their Successors.* East Greenwich, R. I.: Pendulum, 1937. pp. 19-21.

[2] William E. Birkhimer. *Historical Sketch of the Organization, Administration, Material, and Tactics of the Artillery, United States Army.* Washington: James J. Chapman, 1884. pp. 2-17.

[3] Christopher Ward. *The War of the Revolution.* New York: Macmillan, 1952. Vol. I, p. 109.

[4] Charles K. Bolton. *The Private Soldier under Washington.* Port Washington, N. Y.: Kennikat Press, 1964. p. 26.

[5] Birkhimer. *Ibid.* pp. 2-17.

[6] Ward. *Ibid.* p. 221. Carpenter had been a lieutenant in the original United Train.

[7] Francis B. Heitman. *Historical Register of the Officers of the Continental Army.* Washington: 1893. Heitman incorrectly attributes both Carpenter and Crane to Massachusetts. Carpenter was actually the junior "captain-lieutenant", an odd grade between captain and first lieutenant peculiar to the British and American artillery.

[8] Birkhimer. *Ibid.* p. 2-17.

[9] Richards. *Ibid.* pp. 22-27; Anne S.K. Brown. "Rhode Island Uniforms in the Revolution." *Military Collector and Historian*, Vol. X, Spring 1958. pp. 3-5.

Gunner   Matross   Officer

Rhode Island Train of Artillery, 1775

2nd Regiment of Continental Light Dragoons, Dismounted Service, 1780

The 2nd Regiment of Continental Light Dragoons was a Connecticut unit built around a battalion of light horse organized in the summer of 1776 by Major Elisha Sheldon. When four Continental dragoon regiments were authorized by Congress in December of that year, Sheldon was commissioned a Colonel and his battalion passed promptly into the Continental service. The other regiments were not formed until 1777. Consequently, the 2nd Regiment is considered to be the first United States cavalry unit and its "birthday" is observed by Armor and Cavalry units today.

Thanks is due John Trumbull for what little is known of the uniform of the 2nd Light Dragoons. Trumbull is believed to be the creator of a sketch of Major Benjamin Tallmadge; he also painted a delightful miniature of Captain Thomas Young Seymour. Both of these officers were assigned to the Regiment. Trumbull included Seymour on horseback in his painting, "The Surrender of Burgoyne."[1] Care must be used in citing Trumbull as a source for the cut of Revolutionary War uniforms, however, particularly in regard to the collar. He painted some years after the War and invariably shows his subjects in the high collar which did not come into use until 1786 or 1787, and then only among the very fashionable. Trumbull did serve in the War, however, and his portrayal of these dragoons in French-type dragoon helmets with light-blue bands, dark-blue coats faced with buff, and buff small clothes almost certainly represents the regimental dress during much of its service. During the Yorktown campaign, a French officer described Sheldon's Dragoons as wearing white uniforms with black leather helmets with bearskin crests.[2]

In his *Memoir*, Tallmadge describes the organization of the 2nd Light Dragoons in early 1777 and its movements to the end of the War. He writes about the smart appearance of his own troop in June 1777 when it rode off to join the main army under Washington as " . . . composed entirely of dapple gray horses" fitted with black leather bridles and with black bearskin holster covers. In the summer of 1780, he was given "a separate command, consisting of the dismounted dragoons of our regiment and a body of horse" wherewith to harry the British around New York.[3] For this service, the dragoons were formed into two companies of light infantry and appeared to have relished this separate and active type of duty. It is as light infantry that they are shown in this plate, much as they appeared in

their daring exploits at Fort George and at Fort Slongo on Long Island.

For dismounted service of long duration, dragoons in most armies of the period exchanged their heavy boots for infantry footwear and their valises for knapsacks as well as adopting other items of foot equipment. Often, however, they clung to their cavalry helmets and swords. Exactly what Tallmadge's men wore in 1780 is not known — it is probable that no special uniformity prevailed — and the plate depicts what would have been normal equipment. The drummer has replaced the trumpeter of the mounted service. On his drum is the regimental device shown on the blue standard of the unit, its motto being "PATa. CONCITA. FULMnt. NATI." (roughly translated: "When the motherland is aroused, her sons thunder in arms.")[4]

The swords shown are the straight broadswords carried by many regiments of British horse until the period of the Revolution. This pattern was selected because Tallmadge speaks of having "a cavalry fight with broadswords" with some British light dragoons in 1779. Various other types of sabres were also carried by the Continental horse.

Because of the difficulty in securing suitable horses, the 2nd Light Dragoons — and the other three regiments as well — was reorganized as a "legionary corps" of four mounted and two dismounted troops in January 1781, and was assigned to Connecticut's quota for Continental troops. This 2nd Legionary Corps was furloughed in June 1783 and discharged that November. Sheldon was far the most efficient of the four cavalry colonels and his regiment always served with credit.

H. Charles McBarron, Jr.
Frederick P. Todd

[1] The Tallmadge sketch is reproduced in *Ohio Archaeological and Historical Quarterly*, Vol. XVIII, p. 103. The miniature and the original of the surrender painting are in the Yale Gallery of Fine Arts.

[2] Ludwig von Closen. *Revolutionary Journal 1780-1783*. Chapel Hill: Univ. of North Carolina Press. 1958. p. 92.

[3] Benjamin Tallmadge. *Memoir of Col. Benjamin Tallmadge*. New York: T. Holman, 1858. pp. 19-34.

[4] Illustrations of the two surviving standards may be found in: Gherardi Davis. *Regimental Colors in the War of the Revolution*. New York: Gilliss Press, 1907. pp. 12-13. and Frank E. Schermerhorn. *American and French Flags of the Revolution, 1775-1783*. Philadelphia: Pennsylvania Society of the Sons of the Revolution, 1948. pp. 75-79.

2nd Regiment of Continental Light Dragoons, Dismounted Service, 1780

The Provost Company of Light Dragoons, 1778-1783

A resolution of Congress on May 27, 1778 established a "Provost" in the Continental Army — to consist of a captain, four lieutenants, one clerk, a quartermaster sergeant, two trumpeters, two sergeants, five corporals, forty-three provosts, and four "excarboniers" (executioners). This force was to be mounted and accoutered as light dragoons; its mission was to apprehend deserters, rioters, and stragglers. In battle it would be posted in the rear to secure fugitives. The unit, soon styled the "troop of Maréchaussée," after the French term for similar provost troops, was recruited in Pennsylvania. Most of the men had Germanic names; their commander, sometimes termed "Provost Marshal of the Continental Army", was Bartholomew von Heer.[1]

Von Heer's history can be found in Heitman's *Register:* Adjutant to Ottendorff's Battalion, March 19, 1777; Captain, 4th Continental Artillery, April 14, 1777, to rank from March 3; Captain, Provost Company of Light Dragoons, June 1, 1778; Brevet Major, September 30, 1783; served to the close of the war.[2] His company was mentioned occasionally in general orders: it is to be assisted by the regularly detailed provost guard furnished by the various regiments. Lossing notes that "The Maréchaussée was a useful corps. In an encampment it was its business to patrol the camp and its vicinity, for the purpose of apprehending deserters, thieves, rioters, etc., and soldiers who should be found violating the rules of the army. Strangers without passes were to be apprehended by them, and the sutlers in the army were under the control of the commander of the corps. In time of action they were to patrol the roads on both flanks of the army to arrest fugitives and apprehend those who might be skulking away."[3] All of this proves that there is little new in war.

The question of what this company looked like — at least for one period of its existence — is answered by a Hessian prisoner of war, Captain Wiederholdt. While on parole at Reading, Pennsylvania, he noted: "A squadron of Light Dragoons under a German Captain v. Heer, a Bayreuth man, had their winter quarters [1779-80] in Reading. Their uniform was blue coats with yellow facings and vest, leathern breeches, and caskets."[4] "Casket" is undoubtedly "casquett", a visored leather cap or light helmet.

This uniform is shown in this plate. Caps are based on a Revolutionary leather helmet discovered by Company Member Waverly P. Lewis. By customary usage, the trumpeter would be in yellow with blue facings; however, he is shown here in red, since captured British uniform coats were frequently favored for Continental musicians. The prisoner is a deserter from the infantry of Armand's Legion, in the uniform described by Lefferts: "olive colored coatees or jacket, brown breeches, yarn stockings, new shoes."[5]

Information about the Provost Company of Light Dragoons is still scant. One would think that a unit with such natural capabilities for rousing the ire of the individualistic Continental officer and soldier would have left more traces behind it, even if uncomplimentary ones. At first the "provosts" seem to have been picked men, drafted from the entire army, but in July 1781 the Company was placed on the Pennsylvania quota for recruits.

The Company appears to have served without scandal, if not with glory. It was furloughed on June 13, 1783, at camp "near New Windsor," and marched back to Pennsylvania. A small detachment — a sergeant, a corporal, and eight provosts — remained with Washington's headquarters as dispatch riders and orderlies until the following October. So ended the first M.P.'s of American history.

Frederick T. Chapman
John R. Elting

[1] John B. Linn and William Engle. *Pennsylvania in the War of the Revolution.* Harrisburg: L. S. Hart, 1880. Vol. II, pp. 367-368.

[2] Francis B. Heitman. *Historical Register of Officers of the Continental Army During the War of the Revolution, April 1775 to December 1783.* rev. ed. Washington: Rare Book Shop Pub Co., 1914.

[3] Benson J. Lossing. *Pictorial Field-book of the Revolution.* New York: Harper, 1852.

[4] M. D. Learned and C. Grosse, eds. Tagebuch des Capt. Wiederholdt vom 7 Oktober 1776 bis 7 Dezember 1780. New York: n. d.

[5] Charles M. Lefferts. *Uniforms of the American, British, French, and German Armies in the War of the American Revolution, 1775-1783.* New York: New York Historical Society, 1926. p. 87.

Provost   *Officer*

The Provost Company of Light Dragoons, 1778-1783

Captain Robert Mullan's Company, Continental Marines, 1779

When Marines worldwide celebrate the birthday of the United States Marine Corps each November 10, they observe the anniversary of the founding of the Corps by the Congress on that date in 1775 when it resolved:

> That two battalions of Marines be raised, consisting of one Cononel, two Lieutenant Colonels, two Majors, and other officers as usual in other regiments; and that they consist of any equal number of privates with other battalions; that particular care be taken, that no persons be appointed to office, or enlisted into said Battalions, but such are good seamen, or so acquainted with maritime affairs as to be able to serve to advantage by sea when required . . .[1]

After the passage of that resolution, recruiting for the new Corps began in earnest. Probably the most famous of all recruiting rendezvous was the Tun Tavern in Philadelphia. Its proprietor, Robert Mullan, or Mullen, was commissioned a captain in the Continental Marines in June, 1776.[2] Although it does not appear that he went to sea during his career in the Corps, he did see some action with his company in Washington's Trenton-Princeton campaign. The major part of his service was spent commanding the depot company in Philadelphia. Here marines were recruited and trained prior to their assignment to ships of the Continental Navy.

Methods and plans for recruiting marines were quite energetic. A recruiting rendezvous was established in each of the large cities. Offers of prize money, advance money, expense money, pensions — and a promise of an ample grog ration — were presented as an attraction to those who were in a recruiting mood.[3]

"Recruiting parties, attractively uniformed, preceded by drum, fife, and colors, noised their way up and down the streets to excite a thirst for glory and a spirit of military ambition. Occasionally, the party would stop and the officer would harangue the multitude in order to excite their patriotism and zeal for the cause of liberty." The crowd was urged to follow the processions to the rendezvous at the Tun Tavern. "Drumming up" recruits was a literal expression![4]

Benjamin Franklin described such a procession in December 1775:

> I observed on one of the drums belonging to the Marines now raising, there was painted a *Rattlesnake*, with this modest motto under it, 'Don't tread on me.' As I know it is the custom to have some device on the arms of every country, I supposed this may have been intended for the arms of America . . . it occurred to me that the *Rattlesnake* is found in no other quarter of the world besides America and may, therefore, have been chosen on that account to represent her.[5]

Although no description has been found to indicate the color of the background for the insignia, the drum in this plate has a white background to conform with the color of the facings of 1775.

Green was the distinctive color of the Continental Marines' uniform. Officers wore small cocked hats without lace. Following the fashion of the time, they wore their hair long, powdered, clubbed or cued, and dangling almost to the shoulder blade. The green coat had slashed sleeves and pockets. Buttons were of silver with a foul anchor device. The waistcoat was white as were the breeches and thread stockings. A silver epaulette was worn on the right shoulder.[6] Black gaiters were worn as protection when on landing parties. Facings for both officers and enlisted marines were originally white. By 1779, however, facings were changed to red; the exact date and reason for the change are unknown.

The regimentals of enlisted marines in 1779 consisted of a "green coat with red facings, a green shirt, light-colored cloth breeches, white woolen jacket, woolen stockings, and a round hat with white binding."[7] In this plate, both enlisted marines are shown in breeches of imperfectly bleached cloth. A minimum of white buff leather is portrayed because such was difficult to procure. Instead, knapsack straps, for example, are shown in natural-colored leather of the cheapest sort. Buttons were of pewter and carried a foul anchor device.

The green and red uniform appears to have been worn by Continental Marines from 1778 until the end of the Revolution when the Corps was dissolved. There were some exceptions: John Paul Jones, for example, dressed his marines in British-style uniforms of red and white while cruising in European waters.[8] The Marine Corps was formally reestablished in 1798 at which time the uniform became blue faced with red.

H. Charles McBarron, Jr.

[1]*Annals of Congress.* Vol. III, 1775. p. 348.

[2]Clyde H. Metcalf. *A History of the United States Marine Corps.* New York: Putnam's, 1939. p. 12.

[3]Edwin N. McClellan. *History of the United States Marine Corps.* U.S. Marine Corps Historical Section, 1925. Chapter IV, Vol. I, pp. 2-3. Typescript copy in U.S. Army Military History Research Collection, Carlisle Barracks, Pa.

[4]Letter, July 2, 1777, John Paul Jones to Captain Matthew Parke, in: *John Paul Jones Papers.* Vol. I, 1775-1777, as cited by McClellan. *Ibid.* pp. 2-3.

[5]Peter Force. *American Archives.* Fourth Series. Washington, D. C.: 1843. p. 467.

[6]McClellan. *Ibid.* pp. 6-7.

[7]*Pennsylvania Gazette and Weekly Advertiser.* November 10, 1779. Deserter description.

[8]McClellan. *Ibid.* p. 7.

Drummer   Officer   Marine

Captain Robert Mullan's Company, Continental Marines, 1779

Dover Light Infantry Company, Delaware Militia, 1776-1777

The Dover Light Infantry was the uniformed flank company of the Kent County, Delaware, militia in 1776. It was commanded by Thomas Rodney, younger brother of Caesar Rodney, one of Delaware's most prominent Revolutionary War figures. The Company in December 1776 comprised a lieutenant, an ensign, four NCO's, a drummer and a fifer, and twenty-six privates. All had volunteered to march to support George Washington's army on the Delaware River.[1]

On December 14, the little unit left Dover and marched to "the Cross Roads," now Smyrna. At Cristiana Bridge, the men were issued knapsacks and canteens, and three days later they reached Philadelphia, in good health except for some "blistered feet." At Bristol, on the 22nd, the Company joined Brigadier General John Cadwalader's Brigade of Philadelphia Associators, with which it served in the Trenton-Princeton campaign, being consolidated with Captain George Henry's Philadelphia Light Infantry Battalion (or Regiment). In, according to Rodney, "as severe a night as ever I saw [with this] storm of wind, hail, rain and snow," the Dover Light Infantry crossed the Delaware on Christmas night at Dunk's Ferry to cover the disembarkation of the rest of the Brigade.

The crossing, as is well known, was not completed and Cadwalader withdrew his brigade to the Pennsylvania side. Fortunately for our Country, Washington's main crossing, to the north, was brilliantly successful. On the 27th, the brigade tried again; made it; and, with the Light Infantry Battalion (including the Dover Company) as advance guard, marched on Burlington and Bordentown, and eventually to Trenton.

Again serving in the van, the Company made the surprise march on Princeton and played a brave part in the battle there. Following the fight, Rodney was placed in command of the Philadelphia Light Infantry Regiment, and at Morristown, on January 7, 1777, he reported with some pride that the Regiment had been appointed by General Washington "to be his own guard (for the reason I suppose that they had distinguished themselves at Princeton and were the only Regiment in the army that were in complete uniform which was green faced with red)."

On January 14, the Dover Company set off for home, its one month enrollment having expired. These exciting thirty days are, so far as is known, its only claim to fame.

Besides the mention of green coats faced with red, Rodney's diary contains other fragments of information on the appearance of his soldiers. He speaks twice about his "great coat" which he wore during the battle of Princeton. This must have been a civilian model with two or three short capes. Doubtless many of the men (he is careful to point out that they were all gentlemen) carried similar great coats as well as their blankets. Being winter, their leg covering would logically have been overalls.

Among Charles M. Lefferts' notes in the New York Historical Society is a reconstruction he did of the Dover Company's uniform. The headdress he arrived at was the jockey cap shown in this plate. These caps may well have been of a different style, even as ornate as the ones worn by Haslet's Delaware Regiment earlier in 1776, but the simple jockey style is the safest to show without further information.

Each of the light infantry companies on that campaign had "a neat light wagon for their baggage." Rodney took great pride in his wagon and steadfastly refused to turn it over to the brigade quartermaster for a vehicle pool. Probably it was hauled by a single horse led by a soldier or teamster on foot.

The diary of Thomas Rodney is short and well worth reading. This cocky militiaman had seemingly inexhaustible faith and hope in the American cause at a time when it had died out in every other heart but Washington's. He had, furthermore, the ability to encourage others, which he put to good use in those dark days before Trenton.

Clyde A. Risley
Frederick P. Todd

[1] Almost the only source of information on the company is Thomas Rodney's diary, published in the *Papers* of the Historical Society of Delaware, VIII (1888).

Dover Light Infantry Company, Delaware Militia, 1776-1777

Independent Company of Cadets, Massachusetts, 1772-1774

Chartered in 1741 as a volunteer militia company recruited from among the wealthy young men of Boston, the Independent Company of Cadets has a long and honorable record. This plate depicts the uniform of the Company in the years immediately preceding the American Revolution.

John Hancock, already marked by the British for his leadership in revolutionary activities, was the Company's lieutenant colonel commandant at this time. In 1774, the Cadets returned to General Gage the standard he had presented to them and thereby formally indicated their allegiance to the American cause. In the same year, Hancock became president of the first Massachusetts Provincial Congress. The Company was to remain inactive — except for individual members who slipped away from Boston to join the Continental Army — until the British evacuated the city in early 1776. The Cadets then formed the cadre for a Continental regiment. In 1786, the Company was reestablished as a volunteer militia unit.

It was, however, for more innocent and pleasant matters that the Cadets met at the Bunch of Grapes Tavern in the spring of 1772; along with other business, they were going to select a new uniform. The minutes of these meetings are still preserved by the organization and are cited below. It is interesting to note that in spite of its strong Whig sentiment, the Company selected the traditional red of the British foot for its uniforms. The Declaration of Independence was still four years in the future.

> At an Adjournmnt of the Meeting of the Compy Apr. 22, 1772 at the Bunch of grapes
> PRESENT Collo Hancock
> Collo Coffin
> Major Hubbard

The report of the Committee appointed to settle the uniform of the Company being read, A — Motion was made and seconded wether said Report be agreeable to the Company, it was almost unanimously voted in the affirmative and ordered to be recorded —

The Committee appointed to settle the uniform of the Company beg leave to report made the following Report —

FIRST that the pattern of the Cloath be as follows: viz the Coat to be of Scarlet broad Cloth with a narrow Round Cuff and a narrow Lapell of white Cloth, the Lapell to be the length of the waist of the Coat and a fall down Cape the Colour of the Lapell, the Buttons to be plain white Mettle wash'd with silver, the Waistcoat and Breeches to be white with the same Buttons.

SECONDLY that the Hatt be small decorated with a large spangle'd Button and Loop, Silver Loopings, a silver Band and Tossell, and common Cockades.

THIRDLY that the Company appear with white Linnen spatterdashes to be made to come just over the Knee and headed with a broad hem. Allowance must be made above the knee for kneeling, in the firings; to Buckle with a black garter below the knee, the Buttons to be black horn Small and placed at the exact distance of one inch from each other, the Buckles to be of white Mettall.

FOURTHLY that on muster days every Gentln appear with a white Stock and a ruffled shirt the Wiggs and hair to be dressed at the sides club'd behind and well powder'd.

The Uniform Committee promptly found itself in trouble: for some reason, white facings did not suit the rest of the Company. As a result:

> At a Special Meeting calld by order of Collo Hancock & held at the Bunch of Grapes April 27th 1772 —
> PRESENT Collo Hancock
> Collo Coffin
> Maj Hubbard

A number of the Compy having signifid a desire that the Vote pass'd at the last meeting respecting the uniform of the Compy be reconsidered, it was accordingly put to Vote and the Majority was for reconsidering said Vote. A MOTION was then made and seconded that the Uniform to be worn in the Compy should be Scarlet turn'd up with Buff instead of Scarlet and white. A very great Majority was for Scarlet and Buff and the Company was desired to conform themselves accordingly — VOTED that the Waistcoats and Breeches be made agreeable to the report of the Committee except the Color wch must be Buff.

In keeping with British Military practice, the officers carry espontoons; the sergeants, halberds. The sergeant's crimson sash has a central stripe of the unit's facing color, in this case buff. Officers are distinguished by their epaulettes, gorgets, crimson sashes, and swords. It should be noted that an officer saluted while marching by removing his hat.

H. Charles McBarron, Jr.

Independent Company of Cadets, Massachusetts, 1772-1774

Associators of the City and Liberties of Philadelphia, 1775

The Associators of Philadelphia were formed as companies of Volunteer Militia at a meeting in that city November 21, 1747, by Benjamin Franklin and others. The Provincial Congress of Pennsylvania, strongly Quaker, gave the new organization a cautious establishment by announcing on December 7 that these "Proceedings are not disapproved" and that commissions would be issued Associator officers. After the Peace of Aix-la-Chapelle in 1748, interest in militia affairs seems to have waned in Philadelphia, and by 1763 the Associators were greatly reduced in size and importance, if not entirely dormant.[1]

Early in 1775, only two Associator companies are known to have been active: the Philadelphia Greens, Captain John Cadwalader, and the Quaker Blues under Captain Joseph Cowperthwait, then sheriff. But the conflict at Lexington in April of that year led to wildly increased interest, and within a few weeks four uniformed battalions and several separate companies had been formed and were drilling night and day.[2] By August 1775 the Associators of Philadelphia included four infantry battalions (numbered 1st-4th), one rifle battalion (the 5th), an Artillery Battalion, and the City Guards, this last being a sort of auxiliary police force.[3]

Knowledge of the dress of these battalions comes from two letters, one from a Congressman and the other from the wife of a Philadelphia doctor, both written in June 1775. Silas Deane, member of the Second Continental Congress, wrote his wife on June 3:

> The uniform is worth describing to you. It is a dark-brown (like our homespun coat), faced with red, white, yellow, or buff, according to their different battalions, white vest and breeches, white stockings, half-boots, and black knee-garters. The coat is made short, falling but little below the wasitband of the breeches, which shows the size of a man to a great advantage. Their hats are small (as Jessie's little one, almost), with a red, white, or black ribbon, according to their battalions, closing in a rose, out of which rises a tuft of fur of deer (made to resemble the buck's tail as much as possible) six or eight inches high. Their cartouch-boxes are large, with the word LIBERTY and the number of their battalion written on the outside in large white letters. Thus equipped they make a most elegant appearance, as their cartouch-boxes are hung with a broad white horse-leather strap or belt, and their bayonets, etc., on the other side, with the same, which two, crossing on the shoulders diamond-fashion, gives an agreeable appearance viewed in the rear.

> The light infantry are in green, faced with buff; vests, etc., as the others, except the cap, which is a hunter's cap, or a jockey's. These are, without exception, the genteelest companies I ever saw. They have, besides, a body of irregulars, or riflemen, whose dress it is hard to describe. They take a piece of Ticklenbergh, or towcloth, that is stout, and put it in a tanvat until it has the shade of a fallen dry leaf. Then they make a kind of frock of it, reaching down below the knee, open before, with a large cape. They wrap it around them tight on a march, and tie it with their belt, in which hangs their tomahawk. Their hats are the same as the others. They exercise in the neighboring groves, firing at marks and throwing their tomahawks, forming on a sudden into line, and then, at the word, breaking their order and taking their parts to hit their mark. West of this city is a large open square of nearly two miles each way, with large groves each side, in which, each afternoon, they collect, with a vast number of spectators. They have a body of horse in training, but as yet I have not seen them out.[4]

With uncanny accuracy the second letter from Mrs. Mary Morgan to her sister in Baltimore drops the missing pieces into the puzzle:

> Last Thursday we had a grand review of all three battalions all dressed in their regimentals, the first in brown and buff, the 3rd brown turned up with white; and the 2nd brown and red . . . besides their is four other uniforms, the Light Infantry to the 3rd Battalion are dressed in green & with white lappels and white wastcoats, breeches & stockens, smart caps and feathers — it is a compleat a company as can be, all gentlemen and most of them young fellows and very handsome. My neighbor Cadwalider capten and my brother George Morgan first Lieutenant. Their is another company all young Quakers, their uniform is light blue and turned up with white, made exactly like the green. Then their is the Rangers Mr. Frances Capt. Their uniform is tanned shirts with a cape fringed. A belt round their wastes with a Tommy hawk sticking in it. Some of them paint their faces and stick painted feathers in their heads, in short their aim is to resemble Indians as much as possible. Lastly comes the light horse. Mr. Marko their Captain. Their is only five and twenty of them as yet but really they look exceedingly well.[5]

In view of these brown coats faced with different colors it is interesting to recall that on November 4, 1775, the Continental Congress, then sitting in Philadelphia, ordered that the uniforms of the New Continental Army "be dyed brown and the distinctions of the Regiments made in the facings."[6]

Throughout 1775 and 1776 the Associators furnished numerous officers and men to the Pennsylvania battalions of the Continental Line, and in the latter year many of the companies turned out for short tours of duty along the Delaware and elsewhere. They were on active duty throughout the Trenton-Princeton campaign, and fought well, once they had been blooded. Late in 1776, or early in 1777, the Associators were reorganized as the Philadelphia Brigade under Brigadier General Cadwalader, who had earlier commanded the Greens. The name "Associators" does not appear on the rolls thereafter.

H. Charles McBarron, Jr.
Frederick P. Todd

[1]William P. Clarke. *Official History of the Militia and the National Guard of the State of Pennsylvania*. Philadelphia: C. J. Hendleir, 1909. Vol. I, pp. 65-83.

[2]*Ibid*. pp. 83-84; John Thomas Scharf and Thompson Westcott. *History of Philadelphia, 1609-1884*. Philadelphia: L. H. Everts, 1884. Vol. I, pp. 296-97.

[3]*Pennsylvania Archives*, 2d Series, Vol. XIII, pp. 555-764.

[4]Scharf and Westcott. *Ibid*. p. 296.

[5]George E. Hastings. "A Note on 'Miss Keys, a Famous New Jersey Beauty'." *Pennsylvania Magazine of History and Biography*. Vol. LVI, no. 3, 1932. pp. 277-279.

[6]*Journals of the Continental Congress*, Vol. III, p. 323.

5th (Rifle) Battalion

Philadelphia Greens,
Light Infantry Company, 3rd
Battalion

Battalion Companies,
3rd and 2nd Battalions

Associators of the City and Liberties of Philadelphia, 1775

Light Horse of the City of Philadelphia, 1776-1777

Among the oldest United States military units in continuous existence, the Philadelphia Light-Horse was founded by twenty-eight young men of wealth and social distinction on November 17, 1774.[1] Each man agreed to mount, arm, and equip himself at his own expense. One of them, Benjamin Randolph, noted his subsequent purchases — a carbine, a broadsword, belt, cartridge box, pair of pistols, a saddle, gun bucket, saddle bags, saddle cloth, and a "sute" of clothes and cap — in his copy of *Father Abraham's Pocket Almanack-1775*.[2]

The Troop's organization included a captain, first lieutenant, second lieutenant, cornet,[3] quartermaster, two sergeants, and two corporals. A veteran soldier was hired as sword master and riding master; and a trumpeter and a farrier likewise were retained to accompany the Troop on active service.

Volunteering its services early in the Revolution, the Troop's first recorded duty was to escort General George Washington from Philadelphia to New Rochelle on his ride to assume command of the American Army. Throughout the war, detachments of the Troop served as escorts for supply trains and prisoners. In the fall of 1776, the Troop (twenty-five officers and men, plus their trumpeter) was among the Pennsylvania units which reinforced Washington's defeated army on the south bank of the Delaware River. It served with distinction throughout the ensuing Trenton-Princeton campaign, both on reconnaissance missions and several spirited little shock actions. In January 1777, Washington discharged them with sincere thanks. Later, the Troop served in the 1777-1778 operations around Philadelphia.

The exact uniform originally selected was prescribed in the Troop minutes:

> A dark brown short Coat, faced and lined with white; white Vest and Breeches; high topped Boots; round black Hat, bound with silver cord; a buck's tail; and ARMS; a Carbine, a pair of Pistols and Holsters, with flounces of brown cloth trimmed with white; a horseman's Sword; white belts for the sword and carbine.[4]

This is an accurate description except for the hat. Earlier artists, such as Charles M. Lefferts and Henry A. Ogden, pictured the hat as a leather jockey cap, bound at the bottom with silver braid, with a buck's tail mounted from rear to front for a crest.[5] There is, however, a contemporary illustration of the Troop in 1776. James Peale's painting of the battle of Princeton[6] shows an officer wearing what seems to be a jockey cap, but the other members of the Troop in this painting wear definite dragoon helmets, with a frontal plate and light blue turban; their plumes, apparently buck's tails, being attached from front to rear. Peale was an officer in the Philadelphia militia and apparently served at Princeton. Other than these helmets, Peale's depiction of the Troop's uniforms very closely approximates their own original description.[7]

The Troop's horse furniture is described as handsome and expensive: brown edged with white, with white letters "L.H." embroidered on holster flaps and saddle cloths. In Peale's painting, the officer has a brown saddle cloth edged with a lighter stripe, and a red portmanteau. The trooper's saddles are stripped down; holster flaps are of practical bearskin.

Most of the minor discrepancies in various pictures and descriptions of the Troop undoubtedly trace to one fact: this was a self-sustaining organization. While they would attempt to follow English standards of light dragoon fashion, personal preference in such items as boots and saddlery would be inevitable. Difficulties in replacing original clothing and equipment would compound this effect, as would the problems of dressing a "show-horse" outfit for field service. During the Trenton-Philadelphia campaign, the Philadelphia Troop had to be issued "caps," which may very well have been the helmets Peale shows. A turban to protect the back of the neck would have been more than welcome in the freezing Jerseys.[8]

Clyde A. Risley
James P. Simpson
John R. Elting

[1]*History of the First Troop Philadelphia City Cavalry . . .*, Philadelphia: 1875. p. 1. This, together with *History of the First Troop Philadelphia City Cavalry, 1914-1948*, Philadelphia: 1948 — both prepared and published by the command — are the basic sources for this article.

[2]In the Library Company of Philadelphia (Aja/.093).

[3]By special authorization, the Troop — now Troop A, 1st Squadron 223rd Cavalry, Pennsylvania Army National Guard— retains this title for its junior commissioned officer.

[4]*History* (1875), *Ibid.* p. 4; *History* (1948), *Ibid.* p. 190.

[5]*Ibid.*

[6]Peale's original picture is at Yale University and is best known through a crude copy of one of his pupils, William Mercer.

[7]Peale shows coats instead of short jackets; only his officer's coat has white turnbacks, those of the troopers being brown.

[8]*Memorandum Book, Pennsylvania Council of Safety*. January 4, 1777, in *Pennsylvania Archives*, 2d series, Vol. I, p. 495.

Light Horse of the City of Philadelphia, 1776-1777

Colonel Joseph Crockett's Western Battalion, Virginia State Force, 1780-1782

For its internal defense, the Commonwealth of Virginia raised a "line" of state troops distinct from the Virginia Continental Line. Between 1777 and 1782, this force included seven regiments of infantry, one of artillery, one of light dragoons, three legions, and several independent companies and troops. Virginians and others joining the state troops enlisted as regulars for service within the state, were subject to state control, and received from the state bounty, equipment, rank, and pay that was equal to or better than that granted to Continental soldiers. Drafts and entire regiments of these state troops were attached to the Continental Army, and not a few units participated in campaigns far removed from Virginia. As one of the two state infantry regiments organized to protect Virginia's western limits, the Western Battalion was raised by authorization of the State Assembly Act of October 1779. Lieutenant Colonel Joseph Crockett of the 11th Virginia Continental Line Regiment was chosen to lead the battalion, whose ten companies were to be recruited in Boutetourt, Berkeley, and other western counties. A corps of frontier Indian fighters commanded by Major George Slaughter was attached.[1]

By May 27, 1780, the Battalion mustered one lieutenant colonel, one major, six captains, four lieutenants, four ensigns, twelve sergeants, one drummer, and 146 privates.[2] Intended for keeping open George Rogers Clark's lines of communication from Licking Springs westward, Crockett's force was retained in the Eastern Department throughout 1780, bolstering the Convention Guards at Albemarle Barracks and Frederick. Notwithstanding Clark's repeated requests for its services, the Battalion was dispatched in February 1781 as part of a reinforcement for the Southern Army at Guilford Court House, N. C. The Battalion finally joined Clark at Yohogania Court House, now West Virginia, shortly before May 23.[3] Leaving some of the Western Battalion in the vicinity of Fort Pitt, Clark took the rest with him in August 1781 on an anti-Indian campaign. Conditions were so rigorous the battalion ceased to exist by the end of 1781, and its remnants were absorbed into the garrison at the Falls of the Ohio, now Louisville.[4]

As part of the state line, the Western Battalion was accoutered and equipped at Virginia's expense. Governor Thomas Jefferson instructed the Virginia War Office to provide the battalion with clothing, blankets, 170 rifles, "... 1 brass 6-pounder on a travelling carriage compleat, 4 double fortified Iron 4-pounders, 11 Swivels of different sizes."[5] Each man was also to have a leather pouch.[6] This reconstruction of the uniform is based on the type and quantity of cloth drawn by the battalion quartermaster, Major George Walls, from the State Public Store, Richmond, June 22 and August 18, 1780.[7] On June 22, Major Walls signed for:

> To Sundries for Clothing 200 Privates. 609 yards serget for vests, 370 soldiers shoes, 400 pair of soldiers stockings, 200 felt hats, 773 yards oznabrigs for hunting shirts and pockets, 1000 yards oznabrigs for overalls, 300 yards for haversacks, 128 blankets, 1 ounce mohair for the serget;
>
> Sundries for 19 officers: — 25 yards linen, 2½ yards superfine linen for shirts and stocks, 10 pieces nankeens for vests and breeches, 4 pieces jeans and dimothy, 2 pieces Irish linen for facing and pockets for waistcoats and breeches, 2½ pieces cloth for officers, a remnant of red cloth for facings, 1 piece shalloon for the above cloth, 19 hats.

The issue of August 18 consisted of:

> For 200 privates — 8 pieces brown cloth 6/4 wide for 121 coats, 13 pieces ditto for 200 pair breeches = 620 yards, 12½ pieces brown shalloon for facings, 12 pieces oznabrig for lining breeches and sleeves, 40½ yards blue cloth for lapels for 200 coats and 800 dozen pewter, mohair, and metal buttons, 96 yards damaged Russia duck for portmanteaus, 10 hanks sail twine, 8 coils deep sea line.

Peter F. Copeland
Marko Zlatich

[1] William Waller Hening. *The Statutes at Large; Being a Collection of all the Laws of Virginia.* Richmond: 1822. Vol. X, pp. 32, 215.
[2] Julian P. Boyd, ed. *Thomas Jefferson Papers.* Princeton: Princeton Univ. Press, 1950-1956. Vol. III, facing p. 254. As of August 25, 1780, Slaughter's corps had no more than 40 men, all unclothed and ill-equipped. See Colonel John Floyd to Colonel William Preston, in *Wisconsin Historical Collections,* Vol. XXIV, p. 226.
[3] Thomas Jefferson Papers. *Ibid.* Vol. VI, p. 12.
[4] George Rogers Clark Papers. *Illinois Historical Collections.* Vol. VIII, pp. 590, 594.
[5] Thomas Jefferson Papers. *Ibid.* Vol. III, p. 302.
[6] *Ibid.* p. 506.
[7] *Accounts of the Military Store from June 14, 1780 to November 30, 1780,* MS. Archives Division, Virginia State Library.

Field Officer

Sergeant

Private

Private

Colonel Joseph Crockett's Western Battalion, Virginia State Force, 1780-1782

The Minute Battalion of Culpeper County, Virginia, 1775-1776

The Culpeper Minute Battalion consisted of at least ten companies of "regulars" from York and James City Counties. In the fall of 1775 it marched to Williamsburg to join in the expedition against Norfolk where the Royal Governor, Lord Dunmore, was entrenched. Some of these companies thus participated in the Battle of Great Bridge, December 9, 1775.

George Slaughter, one of the members of Captain John Jameson's company, passed on to later generations a description of the assembly of the Battalion prior to its departure for Williamsburg:[1]

> We encamped in Clayton's old field. Some had tents, and others huts of plank & c. The whole regiment appeared according to orders in hunting shirts made of strong, brown linen, dyed the color of leaves of the trees and on the breast of each hunting shirt was worked in large white letters the words 'Liberty or Death!' and all that could procure for love or money [a] buck's tail, wore them in their hats. Each man had a leather belt around his shoulders, with a tomahawk and scalping-knife. The flag had in the center a rattlesnake coiled in the act to strike. Below it were the words 'Don't tread on me!' At the sides, 'Liberty or Death!' and at the top, 'The Culpeper Minute Men' ...The Minute Men were chiefly armed with fowling-pieces and squirrel-guns (rifles) ...

Another appropriate recollection was that of the Battalion's most illustrious member, future Chief Justice John Marshall who as a lieutenant in Captain William Taliaferro's Company, was seen wearing "...a purple or pale blue hunting-shirt and trousers of the same material fringed with white..." and a "...round black hat mounted with a buck's tail for a cockade ..."[2]

While the original sources of these eye-witness accounts can no longer be traced, there is sufficient material in the journals and "day books" of the Williamsburg Public Store to authenticate them in most aspects.[3] These books contain records of purchases and issues of cloth, clothing, and accoutrements for each company. Although space will not permit quoting each issue, an issue to Captain William Taliaferro's company for October 25, 1775, may be considered typical:

26 Yds blue duffil	6/8
8 yds d°	5/8
27 pr Shoes	6/8
2 bound hats	4/6
8½ yds Bearskin	6/3
4 yds German serge	5/–
5 yds Swanskin	2/8

1¾ yds best ditto for Ensign	3/6
4 doz Coat & doz breast buts	5/6
16 Ozs thread	4d
7 Sticks twist 3/1	
18 doz small buts	9/
14 yds Swanskin	3/6

All companies received blue "half-thicks" for enlisted men's leggings and "best blue stroud" for officers' leggings. Other items were oznabrigs for hunting shirts and body shirts, stout duck for pouches, horn buttons for leggings, and oznabrig knapsacks and haversacks.

Individual officers received broadcloth or coating of green, blue, drab, and London brown, which would be suitable for making up into frock coats. For example, on November 14, 1775, Captain William Pickett purchased 1¾ yards of green coating and a dozen coat buttons, and Lieutenants Madison and Taylor 2 yards of light blue coating each on November 6.

A letter from an acting corporal with the battalion in the lines around Norfolk confirms the use of buck's tails as cockades by the early Virginia forces:

> ... all the D--n Torys Down this way are glad to get a bucks tail to putt in their hats now that they may pass for Friends to the Shirt men But you may tell them by their Whegey [sic.] beard and Swarthy Complexion.[4]

As regards the flag, Slaughter's description has stood the test of time, but its actual size, composition, and color are unknown. According to the Williamsburg Public Store records, Captain Taliaferro bought a stand of colors, along with one drum and two fifes, for £6. 6s. 6d. On the same day, eight yards of white shalloon were received for camp colors for the army in Williamsburg. Later on December 13, 1775.... 15 taffeta colors, 15 tassils and cords, 15 spears & c...." were purchased from William Lux & Co., merchants of Baltimore.

Peter F. Copeland
Marko Zlatich

[1] Raleigh Travers Green. *Geneological and Historical Notes on Culpeper County, Virginia, Embracing a Revised and Enlarged Edition of Dr. Philip Slaughter's History of St. Mark's Parish.* Culpeper: 1900. Part Second, p. 13.

[2] John F. Dillon. *John Marshall, Life, Character and Judicial Services.* Chicago: Callaghan & Co., 1903. Vol. III, p. 15, 287-288.

[3] Williamsburg Public Store, *Daybook,* October 12, 1775-October 17, 1776, MS in Division of Archives, Virginia State Library.

[4] William B. Wallace to James Wallace, Bachelor's Mill, March 4, 1776, Box 2 *Wallace Family Papers,* No. 38-150, Alderman Library, University of Virginia.

Private Man

Officer Captain Taliaferro's Co.

Private Man

Officer Captain Wm. Pickett's Co.

The Minute Battalion of Culpeper County, Virginia, 1775-1776

French Regiments at Savannah, 1779

A preliminary word on the organization of the French army at the seige of Savannah will explain why this plate shows several regiments, rather than one unit. This force of some 3750 men, commanded by Admiral Comte Charles d'Estaing, consisted of drafts and detachments of less than battalion strength for 80 days' service from various regiments garrisoning the following islands in the French Indies:

Martinique — 750 men from the Viennois, Champagne, Auxerrois, and La Martinique Regiments, and some artillerists; Guadeloupe — 850 from the La Guadeloupe, Armagnac, and La Martinique Regiments and some artillerists; St. Dominique — 1500 from the Cap, Gâtinois, Agenois, Cambrésis, and Port-au-Prince Regiments and 600 from the Foix and Haynault Regiments. The plate, therefore, attempts to convey the spirit of chaos which brought disaster to an army arranged into provisional units that never before had served together and were commanded by officers who were strangers.

In order to portray more faithfully the appearance of these troops at Savannah, the uniforms chosen are not those of the Ordonnance of 1779, which at that time existed only on paper. Admiral d'Estaing's troops had been away from France for considerable periods, and therefore wore the dress prescribed in 1776-1777. During this period, all French infantry wore white breeches and waistcoats. Either white or black gaiters could be worn depending on which pair had worn out first. In theory, the stocks were white, but black ones were frequently favored in spite of the Musée de l'Armée documentation to the contrary.[1]

Regimental distinctions depicted are:

1st Lieutenant, *Régiment du Cap* — light blue 1772 — pattern coat, faced Saxon green; white buttons stamped with an anchor, denoting this as one of the four colonial regiments in the *Corps Royal de la Marine* (Navy); two silver epaulets with red silk zigzag line to indicate rank; gilt gorget with the arms of France and an anchor in silver; cartridge box plate the same.

Mùlatto drummer, *Régiment du Cap* — regulation coat of royal livery, blue faced red; pockets, button holes, seams, and sleeves laced crimson with a white patterns; the green hoops on the brass drum are the only regimental distinction; black felt hat, white lace and cockade.

2nd Captain, Walsh's Irish Regiment — red coat, 1776 — pattern with a small standing collar; piped, cuffed and lapelled blue; five gold-laced button holes on sleeves; plain black hat, black and white cockade affixed by a gold loop and button; gilt epaulets have two red stripes to indicate rank and short fringes of mixed gold and red threads; regulation gorget; officer's small cartridge box; armed with fuzee, short bayonet, and sword with gilt hilt.

Chasseur, *Régiment d'Armagnac* — white coat, yellow collar, sky-blue cuffs and lapels, white buttons; black felt hat, white lace and cockade, green plume; short brass-hilted sword.[2]

Grenadier, *Régiment d'Haynault* — bearskin cap, brass plate with royal arms, white cap cord, white plume topped crimson; grey-white coat, yellow standing collar, crimson cuffs and lapels, white epaulets with crimson linen fringes, yellow buttons. Like the chasseur, he has a short infantry sword but apparently has lost his musket.

Fusilier, *Régiment de Champagne* — silver-grey collar, lapels, and cuffs; yellow buttons; white hat lace and cockade; single shoulder belt to support both cartridge box and bayonet frog.

Despite the makeshift character of this force, the French fought bravely. Unfortunately, d'Estaing's arrogance plus an American traitor who deserted to the British with warning of the timing of the final Franco-American assault made their courage fruitless.

Eugene Leliepvre
Marcel Baldet

[1] The main sources used for this plate are: Louis Susane. *Histoire de l'Armée Francaise*. Paris: 1876, 5 Vols.; Viscomte de Noailles, *Marins et Soldats Francais en Amérique*. Paris: 1903; contemporary watercolors in the Musee de l'Armée, Paris; and the Royal Ordonnances and Regulations of 1772, 1776, 1777, and 1779.
[2] A watercolor in the Musée de l'Armée collection shows that the plume consisted of three feathers; however, the specimen worn by the chasseur displays the ravages of a hard campaign.

Chasseur, Armagnac   Grenadier, Hainault   Fusilier, Champagne
Drummer, du Cap   Officer, du Cap   Officer, Walsh   Sergeant, Guadeloupe

French Regiments at Savannah, 1779

The Soissonnais Infantry, 1780-1783

The Soissonnais Regiment sailed from Brest in April 1780 as part of Lieutenant General Comte de Rochambeau's expeditionary force. Most French regiments of the period had two five-company battalions. One company of the 1st Battalion were grenadiers; one of the 2nd Battalion, "chasseurs" or light infantrymen. The remaining eight companies were classified as "fusiliers" or musketeers. Grenadiers and chasseurs were elite troops, especially the former. As such, they carried a short saber in addition to musket and bayonet.

The Regiment was splendidly outfitted according to the new uniform regulations of 1779 which gave the regiment uniforms with crimson facings and yellow buttons stamped with the number "41". Pockets of the uniform were horizontal.

Although German and Italian regiments in French service wore various shades of blue, and the Swiss and Irish had red coats, the native French regiments wore white uniforms. Under the coat, soldiers had a long-sleeved waistcoat. White gaiters were worn with full dress; black gaiters on field service. Both types were long with twenty to twenty-four buttons down the side. Garters were worn just below the knee.

The 1779 regulations also specified a black "three-corned" hat, edged with black worsted lace, and with a white cockade on its left front. After the Expeditionary Force arrived in America, a black-and-white cockade was adopted in recognition of the Franco-American alliance. Grenadiers preferred their old bearskin "bonnets" to the cocked hat and continued to wear them — in the Soissonnais Regiment, with a brass cap plate, a white cap cord, and a white-and-crimson plume. After the informal 18th Century practice of regiments providing their own uniforms, and because their colonels were men of influence at court, authorities often ignored such violation of instructions.

For summer duty and for drill, troops wore the waistcoat without the coat. The chasseur in the left background of the plate is shown in drill dress, and the forage cap or "pokalem". The pokalem's side flaps could be turned down over the ears in bad weather. Its front was decorated with a distinctive device for each company, in this case the hunting horn of the chasseurs. In very warm weather, even the grenadiers might put aside their bearskins for the despised cocked hat.

By regulation, grenadiers were to wear red shoulder straps, chasseurs green, and fusiliers white, each piped with the regimental color. In practice, the grenadiers continued to wear their pre-1779 red epaulettes and the chasseurs decorated themselves with completely non-regulation green ones. Coat skirt ornaments were in the regiment's facing color; fleurs-de-lis for the fusiliers, flaming grenades for the grenadiers, and hunting horns for the chasseurs.

Drummers' coats were royal blue faced with the regimental color and liberally decorated with "royal lace," crimson with a white chain design. The drum shells were plain brass and the wooden hoops, blue.

Officers uniforms were cut like those of the enlisted men but made of better material. In the Soissonnais Regiment, the buttons and other metal were gold. Officers' rank was indicated by their epaulettes which were gold with an intermixture of bright-red silk threads, the proportion of red decreasing as the officer's rank increased. Sword knots were gold and red in the same proportions. On duty, infantry officers wore gold-plated gorgets, ornamented with the arms of France in silver. Non-commissioned rank was indicated by stripes around the forearm just above the cuff. The chasseur's chevron in the plate is a service stripe.

French infantry were armed, at least in theory, with the "Charleville" musket, Model 1777, caliber .69. This weapon, however, differed but little from earlier models of 1763-1774, many of which remained in service.

Each regiment had a "Colonel's Color" and one "Ordonnance" or regulation flag for each company. These flags had no national significance since the traditional white Bourbon banner with gold fleurs-de-lis was not officially adopted until 1789. The white cravate, or streamer flown from the pike head, however had been a French rallying sign from the time of Henri IV.

Most infantry regimental colors were divided into cantons by a central white cross. The Soissonnais Regiment had an all-white colonel's color with the central cross indicated only by seams. Its ordonnance flags had their cantons divided into red and black triangles. As with most French regiments, these colors had no relationship to regimental facings; their original significance is almost unknown today.

As a minor historical jest, Americans remembered the Soissonnais as having beautiful "rose-colored" facings. The crimson dye for facings and plumes had apparently been unstable and was badly faded by the time the Regiment marched through Philadelphia enroute to Yorktown in September 1781. A detachment of the Soissonnais had been serving in the West Indies since 1779 and had not been issued the new-model uniforms. When it rejoined the regiment, its personnel were still wearing the pre-1779 uniform — white with red cuffs and facings flecked with white, and a sky-blue collar.

Eugene Leliepvre
John R. Elting

Chasseur in drill uniform   *Ensign and Regimental Color*   *Field Officer in undress [Tenue de ville]*

Fusilier in field uniform   *Genadier Corporal in full dress*   *Drummer in full dress*

The Soissonnais Infantry, 1780-1783

French Expeditionary Corps, Rochambeau's Staff, 1780-1783

On March 1, 1780, the King of France signed the appointment of Lieutenant General Jean Baptiste de Vimeur, Comte de Rochambeau, to command the Expeditionary Corps which was to leave for North America. His instructions stressed that the Comte de Rochambeau would be under the command of General George Washington to whom would be accorded the honors due a Marshal of France, and that he would work out plans for military operations in agreement with Washington. Nevertheless, French troops were to be employed as a national unit under French commanders.

Rochambeau's Corps totalled slightly over 5000 officers and men. It included four infantry regiments — Bourbonnais, Soissonnais, Saintonge, and Royal Deux-Ponts, the "Legion of Lauzun" consisting of 300 hussars and 300 infantrymen, and the Royal Corps of Artillery of Auxonne which had 500 artillerymen and 26 artificers.

In this plate, grouped around the Comte de Rochambeau, are some of the members of his staff. Rochambeau wears the undress uniform of a lieutenant general: blue coat, lined with blue and ornamented down the front with twelve gold buttons and gold embroidery in a spiral ribbon pattern. The same embroidery edges the standing collar, and a double row of embroidery and three buttons garnish each of the round cuffs. The horizontal pockets have four rows of embroidery and three buttons. Vest and trousers are of white dimity. In full-dress uniform, the embroidery was wider; the trousers and vest scarlet, and ornamented with the same gold embroidery. Rochambeau wears a red ribbon across his shoulder and an eight-pointed, silver-edged cross on his coat, the insignia of the Grand Cross of the Order of St. Louis which he had received in 1771.

At his right is the Comte Hans Axel von Fersen, a Swedish officer attached with the rank of lieutenant colonel to the Royal Deux-Ponts Regiment. The French Army of this period had a large surplus of officers. Many of these could by only "attached" to some unit, which they were encouraged not to annoy with their presence. Deux-Ponts was a mercenary unit recruited out of the dominions of the Bishop of Liege. Fersen's coat is deep sky-blue, with lemon-yellow facings and cuffs, and silver buttons. His epaulettes are silver with heavy "bullions," their straps decorated with two red silk cords, the insignia of his grade.

At Fersen's right is a colonel of the Royal Artillery Corps; his royal blue coat has scarlet cuffs and scarlet linings to its coat tails. A cording of the same color outlines its horizontal pockets and facings. Vest and trousers are blue, buttons gilt. The gold epaulettes are those of his grade.

In front of the artillery officer kneels an aide-de-camp, Louis-Alexandre Berthier, future Marshal of France and Napoleon's chief of staff. At this time, he served as "Sous-Aide Marechal-des-Loges," with the grade of colonel. This title, like many others, defies exact translation; it indicates an assistant to the Expeditionary Corps' chief of staff. Berthier wears a royal blue coat, lined with blue, with a standing collar and round cuffs. The coat is ornamented by eight gold-embroidered buttonholes across its front, two on each cuff, and three on each pocket. The trousers and vest are scarlet, the latter with a dozen small buttons and light embroidery down its front and on its pockets. Officers on this duty wore epaulettes and sword knots of their respective grades.

At Rochambeau's left is an engineer officer. His coat is royal blue with black velvet cuffs and facings and with a red lining. This lining extends slightly above the collar, forming an edging. The vest and trousers are scarlet.

In the left rear of the group is a Commissaire des Guerres, another title impossible to translate literally. (Commissaires were civilian officials who handled supply, evacuation, transport, and other service and administrative functions.) He wears a coat of dark iron-grey with a standing collar and scarlet lining; the coat has ten gilt buttons and is embroidered with a pattern of acanthus leaves. His sword has a silver guard and a gold sword knot trimmed with threads of blue and red silk.

With the Commissaire stands an officer of the Royal Navy. His coat is royal blue, lined with scarlet; the vest and trousers are also scarlet. He wears gilt buttons; his hat, gold laced; and his sword knot is gold.

In the rear center is a hussar of Lauzun's Legion, serving as a courier. His dolman is deep sky-blue with white lace and braiding and white bullet buttons. His Hungarian-style trousers are lemon-yellow, trimmed with white braid. His "barrelled" sash is yellow with red slides. The black felt shako is trimmed with yellow lace.

Behind Rochambeau stands a Marechal-de-Camp; an officer of this grade ranked directly below a lieutenant general and wore the same uniform but with one less row of embroidery on the cuffs and pockets.

Finally, at the right rear is an officer of the Corps of Topographical Engineers (Ingenieurs-Geographies). He wears a royal blue coat, lined with white, with "aurore" (roughly translated as a yellowish-orange) cuffs, collar, and facings. The front of the coat is ornamented with seven silver-embroidered buttonholes; its round cuffs have three buttonholes with silver embroidery, as do its vertical pockets. The hat has a silver binding; the sword has a silver hilt and sword knot.

As a visible sign of the Franco-American alliance, Rochambeau had a small black cockade superimposed upon the normal white cockade of the French Army, black being the cockade worn by the Americans.

Eugene Leliepvre
Marcel Baldet

Commissaire des Guerres

Aide de Camp
Army Staff Corps

Naval Officer

Field Officer
Royal Artillery

Hussar, Lauzun Legion

Field Officer,
Royal Deux Ponts Regiment

Marechal de Camp

Lieutenant
General

Topographical
Engineer Officer

Field Officer
Engineers

French Expeditionary Force, Rochambeau's Staff, 1780-1783

THE POST REVOLUTIONARY WAR PERIOD, 1783-1795

United States Regular Units

New York Militia

The U.S. Battalion of Artillery, 1786-1794

The Battalion of Artillery was authorized by the Act of October 20, 1786, by which Congress tried hastily to increase the size of the tiny Federal establishment from 700 to 2040 men, plus officers, in order to deal with Shay's Rebellion in Massachusetts.[1]

Of the projected battalion of artillery, two companies were already in existence and on active service. These were the artillery companies, from Pennsylvania and New York respectively, which formed an organic part of the mixed First American Regiment under Lieutenant Colonel Commandant Josiah Harmar. The New York company, commanded by Captain John Doughty, had originally been raised in early 1776 by Alexander Hamilton; in 1786, it was the only unit with unbroken lineage from the Revolutionary War.

Under the Act of October 20, 1786, John Doughty became Major Commandant of Artillery. His command consisted of the two artillery companies — Captain William Ferguson's Pennsylvanians and the New Yorkers now under Captain James Bradford — of the First American Regiment plus two companies raised in Massachusetts by Captains Henry Burbeck and Joseph Savage. On January 30, 1787, the War Office officially constituted the Battalion of Artillery and prescribed its uniform:

> Hats cocked — Yellow trimmings — Coats Blue Scarlet Lappels, cuffs and standing cape — length of the Coat to reach to the Knee, Scarlet linings and Yellow Buttons — Vests white with short flaps three buttons on each pocket — Overalls — Cockades of black leather round with points four inches diameter — Shoulder straps — Blue edged with red on both Shoulders — Feathers — Black and red tops to rise Six Inches above the brim of the Hat — Epaulettes — The Officers Gold — The Major 2 a single row of bullion — Capts 1 Epaulette on the right shoulder 2 rows of bullion — the Lieuts 1 Epaulette on the left shoulder 1 row of bullion — Sergts 2 Epaulettes Yellow Worsted — Corporals 1 Epaulette right shoulder. Swords — Sabre form, Yellow Mounted — The Majors 3 feet & Capts & Subs 2½ feet.
> The Uniform of the Music to be red found with blue.[2]

Artillerymen were armed, equipped, and frequently served as infantry. This plate shows them in full dress, their hair powdered. The bearskin covers on their knapsacks, a distinction inherited from the First American Regiment, were both strong and waterproof. The matross's cap is the type that apparently replaced the cocked hat during campaigns.

Ferguson's and Bradford's companies remained on the Ohio, attached to Harmar's Regiment. Burbeck's and Savage's Companies initially garrisoned West Point and Springfield Arsenal respectively, and in 1790 were sent to Georgia to guard the frontier of Spanish East Florida.

The troops on the Ohio encountered uniform problems as early as 1788. Harmar, now brevet brigadier general, wrote Secretary Knox: "I observe that the overalls are to be all blue — I am sorry it was out of your power to have white cloth procured — White overalls in my opinion are more Military." Two months later Harmar reiterated: ". . . I have to request that you will be pleased to order in future, that the Clothing shall be made as follows, Viz. — *Cocked Hats, Long Coats* & *White* Under Dress — The Regiment being thus clothed will certainly cut an infinitely more martial appearance than it does at present . . ."[3]

Ferguson's and Bradford's companies took part in Harmar's indecisive Indian campaign of 1790; and in early 1791, Ferguson succeeded Doughty as Major Commandant of Artillery. Ferguson and Bradford were killed and the two companies almost annihilated in St. Clair's defeat by the Miamis in November 1791. When Anthony Wayne organized the Legion of the United States in 1792, the artillery companies in Georgia, much reduced in strength, were called to the northwest frontier, and Henry Burbeck, now the senior captain, was appointed Major Commandant. On August 20, 1794, the four artillery companies took part in the famous Battle of Fallen Timbers.

Shortly thereafter, pursuant to the Act of May 9, 1794, the Battalion of Artillery was absorbed by the newly-authorized Corps of Artillerists and Engineers, consisting of four battalions of four companies each. Most of this organization was assigned to the new coastal fortifications rather than to the Legion's field forces. The Artillery uniform remained unchanged; one account in 1799 describes officers as wearing "yellow leather breeches."[4]

H. Charles McBarron, Jr.
Lt. Col. Arthur P. Wade.

[1] *Journals of the Continental Congress*, XXXII, pp. 255-6.
[2] Extracts from an Orderly Book of the United States Army 1786-1800. These extracts are the property of Chandler Smith of New York City. Copies are in the U.S. Military Academy Library, West Point, N.Y.
[3] Harmar Letter Book "B"; Harmar Letter Book "C". In the William L. Clements Library, Ann Arbor, Michigan.
[4] Rene Chartrand. "First Regiment, Artillerist and Engineers, Fort Machinac, 1799." *Military Collector & Historian*. Vol. XXIV, Fall 1973. p. 158.

Drummer   Matross   Sergeant   Lieutenant   Captain

The U.S. Battalion of Artillery, 1786-1794

Infantry of the Legion of the United States, 1794

From 1792 to 1796, the United States Army was officially designated "The Legion of the United States." Its organization was based upon that of the classic Roman legion, the Secretary of War Henry Knox and Major General Anthony Wayne, its commander, having begun their military educations with Julius Caesar's *Commentaries.* The Legion was to have a total strength of 5120 officers and men, exclusive of Wayne and his staff, and to consist of eight battalions of infantry, four battalions of riflemen, one battalion (four troops) of light dragoons, and one battalion (four companies) of artillery. These were grouped into four "sublegions", each consisting of two battalions of infantry and one of riflemen. The dragoons and artillery were assigned to the sublegions or employed separately as the situation required.

The 1st and 2nd sublegions were formed from the existing 1st ("American") and 2nd Infantry Regiments, both of which had suffered heavily during previous unsuccessful Indian campaigns. Because of the difficulty of securing recruits, the Legion never reached its authorized strength, and the 3rd and 4th Battalions of riflemen were not formed. This was partially redeemed by the organization of an elite light infantry company in each infantry battalion, and by Wayne's insistence upon individual marksmanship. During 1794, additional artillerymen were authorized.

The Legion was the equivalent of the division of all arms which the French Army was then developing as a self-sufficient tactical organization. Its high proportion of riflemen and light infantry was specifically designed for frontier warfare. With it, Wayne broke the Indian tribes of the "Old Northwest" in his masterful Fallen Timbers campaign of 1794, enabling the United States to nudge the British out of the frontier posts they still held in the Northwest territory. After Wayne's death, his incompetent successors abandoned the legionary organization for the more conventional — and more rigid — regimental system. Nevertheless, despite its brief existence, the Legion of the United States remains unquestionably one of the most effective military forces in all American history.

An unusually competent, forceful, and imaginative commander, Wayne understood how much a smart uniform contributed to the individual soldier's self-respect and to unit morale. On September 11, 1792, he issued the following order:

> The officers being arranged to the four Sub Legions, it now becomes expedient to give those Legions distinctive Marks, which are to be as follows — Viz —
>
> The first Sub Legion white Binding upon their Caps, with white plumes and Black hair —
>
> The Second Sub Legion Red binding to their Caps,

red plumes, with White hair.

> The third Sub Legion — Yellow binding to their Caps — Yellow plumes and Black Hair.
>
> The fourth Sub Legion — Green binding to their Caps, with Green Plumes and white hair . . .

On the following day, further orders were issued:

> . . . The Officers will wear plain Cock'd Hats with no other distinctive marks but the plumes of their respective Sub Legions, except in actual service or action, when they will wear the same caps with the Non Commissioned officers and Privates of the respective Sub Legions.[1]

Later orders included instructions that the tails of cattle slaughtered were to be used "to complete the Caps of the Soldiery." The headdress was consistently called a "cap," and it carried a mane of white or black hair, probably fairly long. It is clear that what was described was a light infantry cap of one of the styles used during the Revolutionary War.

It was, more than likely, cut from a cocked hat and had an upright front piece or flap — or possibly two such flaps — of felt with variously colored binding sewed around the edges. The Light Company soldier in this plate wears such a cap.

At some date between 1792 and 1794, the style of infantry headdress was changed to a "round" hat with a strip of bearskin across the crown. In the plate, the second soldier wears the newer headdress. The officer wears his coat buttoned across his chest; it could be arranged at will to conform to the style shown for the men.

Several devices worn by modern U.S. Army regiments saw their beginning in the Legion. The 1st Infantry shows the upper right of its shield in red in honor of the plumes and other red devices it carried as the 2nd Sub Legion. The crest of the 3rd Infantry's coat of arms is an officer's cocked hat with a white plume for the 1st Sub Legion, the ancestral unit of the present 3rd Infantry. The green center stripe in the shoulder loop of the 4th Infantry was taken from the green of the 4th Sub Legion although these two units have no relationship. Both the 1st and 3rd Infantry Regiments carry the battle honor MIAMI for their participation in the Fallen Timbers campaign as units of the Legion of the United States.

H. Charles McBarron, Jr.
Frederick P. Todd
John R. Elting

---

[1]"General Wayne's Orderly Book, 1792-1797." in: Michigan Pioneer and Historical Society *Collections.* Vol. XXXIV, 1904, pp. 341-733. A MS copy exists in the National Archives, RG 98, Book 168, Post-Revolutionary Collection.

Private, Light Infantry Company,
1st Sublegion

Captain,
2nd Sublegion

Sergeant, Battalion Company,
4th Sublegion

Infantry of the Legion of the United States, 1794

New York City Legion, New York Militia, 1786-1799

In 1795 the militia, uniformed and otherwise, of New York County (the Island of Manhattan) comprised the 1st and 2nd Troops of Horse, the more or less independent Regiment of Artillery, and the Brigade. This last command consisted of the Brigade Company of Artillery and five regiments of militia, each of these regiments having two uniformed flank companies of light infantry or grenadiers and eight or more non-uniformed companies of common militia. As early as 1786, in a process which was to continue for a half century, the uniformed flank companies had separated themselves from the rabble of common militia and formed a separate command called the City Legion. In 1799, this became the 6th Regiment of Infantry, and, in 1805, was brought fully into the uniformed militia as the 2nd Regiment, New York State Artillery.[1]

The City Legion during the inauguration of President George Washington in 1789 contained:

"New York Grenadiers (Captain George Harsen), dressed in 'blue coats with red facings and gold lace broideries, cocked hats with white feathers, and white waistcoats and breeches, and black spatterdashes, buttoned close from the shoe to the knee.' According to one description, they were organized 'in the imitation of the guard of the great Frederick, of only the tallest and finest-looking young men of the city.'

"German Grenadiers (Captain George Scriba), dressed in 'blue coats, yellow waistcoats and breeches, black gaiters, and towering cone-shaped caps, faced with bearskin.'

"Scotch Infantry (its commander so far unidentified), 'in full highland costume, with bagpipes.'[2]

"Five or more uniformed companies of light infantry; and the *Brigade Company of Artillery* (Captain John Van Dyek), in blue uniforms faced with red."[3]

Over the next six years the organization remained much the same, except for the possible disappearance of the Scotch Infantry. Some pictures of the Legion's uniform for this period have been located. About 1795 an artist, believed to be William Dunlap, painted a portrait of Lieutenant Colonel David Van Horne, Adjutant General of New York, inspecting the Legion. The troops, shown dimly in the background, have blue coats faced with a rather light red, blue miter-shaped hats, and white crossbelts.[4] Portraits of Lieutenant

Colonel Richard Varick, in blue faced white, and of Lieutenant Colonel Gerard Studdiford, in blue faced red, also exist; both were field officers of the Brigade.[5] A reconstruction of the dress of an officer of the German Grenadiers exists in the New York Historical Society. Finally there is the fascinating contemporary watercolor by an unknown artist in the Henry Francis duPont Winterthur Museum, which shows cavalry, artillery, grenadiers, light infantry, and field music, and is titled "New York Militia." Although not identified as being the City Legion, no other body of New York troops of this period fits the companies illustrated.[6]

The leftmost figure in this plate is that of Lieutenant Colonel Van Horne. His uniform, taken from his portrait, is the blue coat with red facings and yellow metal of the state artillery. The grenadier is based on a combination of sources. The New York Historical Society shows his coat as very light blue, faced with a very light straw-color. The same shade is used in his vest and breeches; his metal is yellow. If the respective positions of the lieutenant colonel and sergeant appear informal, it should be remembered that they were fellow gentlemen volunteers. The red coat of the drummer and the blue jacket of the light infantryman are from the Winterthur watercolor, which suggests that the flank companies wore either red or white facings, and that all musicians wore red faced with blue. A note on New York militia cap plates by COMPANY Fellow J. Duncan Campbell appeared in the *Military Collector and Historian*, March, 1950, pp. 8-9.

H. Charles McBarron, Jr.
John R. Elting
Frederick P. Todd

[1] New York State Historian. *Military Minutes of the Council of Appointments of the State of New York*, 1783-1821. Albany: 1901-1902. 3 Vol., passim; Emmons Clark. *History of the Seventh Regiment of New York, 1806-1889*. New York: The Regiment, 1890. 2 Vol. pp. 28-35; Asher Taylor. *Recollections of the Early Days of the National Guard*. New York: Bradstreet & Son, 1868. passim.

[2] Rufus W. Griswold. *The Republican Court*. New York: D. Appleton, 1885. p. 139; *New York Daily Advertiser*. April 24, May 1, 1789.

[3] *Military Uniforms in America*, Plate No. 8, 1949.

[4] In 1954, this portrait was owned by Mr. Victor Spark of New York City.

[5] The former is in the Albany Institute of History and Art, and the latter in the Museum of the City of New York.

[6] Catalog No. 57.1146.A.

Adjutant General
New York Militia

Sergeant
German Grenadiers

Drummer

Artilleryman
Brigade Company of Artillery

Light Infantryman

New York City Legion, New York Militia, 1786-1795

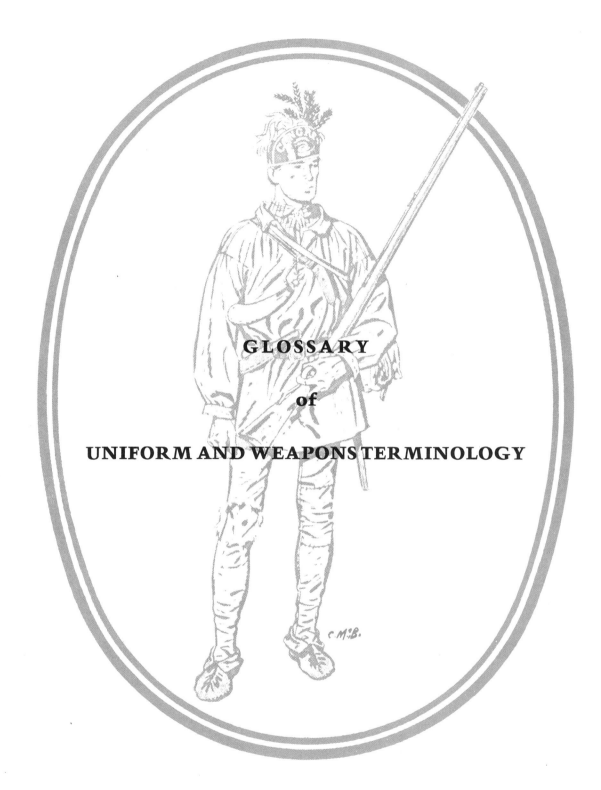

GLOSSARY

of

UNIFORM AND WEAPONS TERMINOLOGY

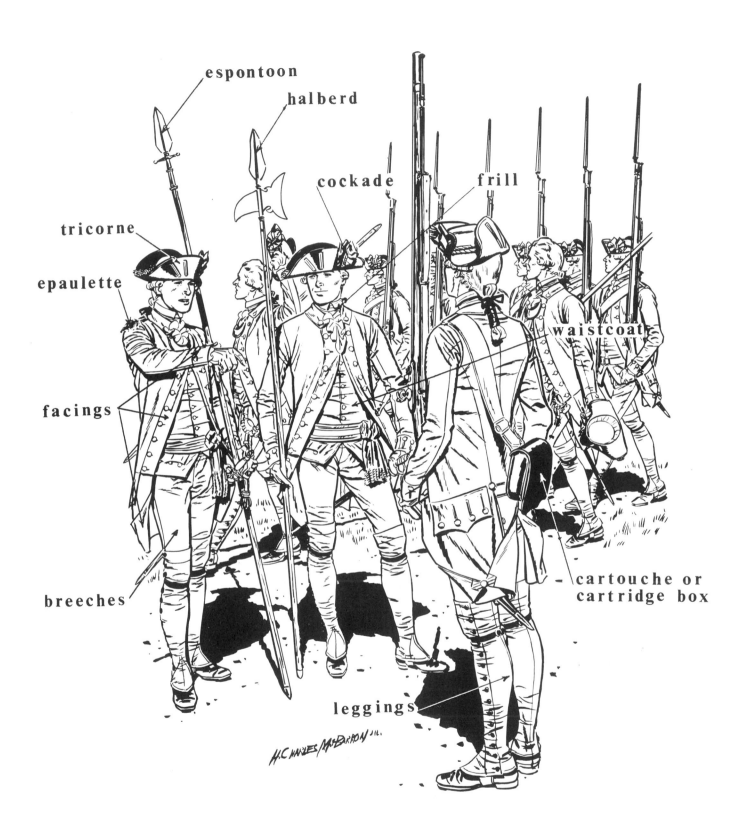

espontoon

halberd

cockade

frill

tricorne

epaulette

waistcoat

facings

breeches

cartouche or
cartridge box

leggings

Uniforms of the Revolutionary War Period

Glossary

(Editor's Note: To provide a contemporary description of uniform details, accoutrements, and weapons, Charles James' *A New and Enlarged Military Dictionary, or Alphabetical Explanation of Technical Terms* . . ., London: T. Egerton, 1802, has been used for many of the terms defined in this glossary. Those taken from James are in italics; those prepared by the editors, in standard type face.)

A

AIGUILLETTES, Fr. tagged points, such as hang from the shoulders in military uniforms, particularly among the Russians, Prussians, &c.

ARTIFICER or Artificier, he who makes fire-works, or works in the artillery laboratory, who prepares the fuzes, bombs, grenades, &c. It is also applied to the military smiths, collarmakers, &c. &c. and to a particular corps. Artificers, in a military capacity, are those persons who are employed with the artillery in the field, or in the arsenals; such as wheelers, smiths, carpenters, collar-makers, coopers, tinmen, &c.

B

BATTALION, the major subdivision of a regiment. In the period of the Revolution, "battalion" and "regiment" were practically synonymous.

BATTALION COMPANIES, those companies of a battalion, normally seven or eight in number, which were neither grenadiers nor light infantry.

BELTED PLAID, the ancient garb of the Scotch Highlanders, and still worn by some of our Highland regiments. The belted plaid consists of twelve yards of tartan, which are plaited, bound round the waist by a leathern belt, the upper part being attached to the left shoulder.

BICORNE, a 2-cornered cocked hat.

BOMBARDIERS, non-commissioned officers so called because they were chiefly employed in mortar and howitzer duty. They are to load them on all occasions; and in most services they load the shells and grenades, fix the fuzes, prepare the composition both for fuzes and tubes, and fire both mortars and howitzers on every occasion.

BULLION, gold or silver lace. See LACE.

C

CAMP COLORS, small flags, approximately 18 inches square, used to mark the camp site of a regiment. Normally these flags were the color of the regiment's facings and were marked with its number or name.

CAPE, a common name for a coat collar.

CAPOT (Capote and various other spellings), a French term for an overcoat, often with an attached hood.

CARTOUCHE (Cartouche box, cartridge box), generally a leather pouch enclosing a wooden block with holes bored in it to hold individual cartridges. The number of holes varied, but between 20 and 30 were standard.

CARTRIDGE, a prepared round of ammunition; a ball and a charge of powder wrapped in a twist of tough paper.

CHASSEURS, Fr. Light infantry men, forming a select body upon the left of a battalion, in the same manner that grenadiers are posted on the right. They must be particularly active, courageous, and enterprizing.

* *COCKADE, a ribbon worn in the hat. We have already observed, that this military mark succeeded the scarf which was formerly worn by officers and soldiers belonging to European nations, and which are principally distinguished in the following manner. In the army and navy of Great Britain, black silk ribbon for officers, and hair cockades for the non-commissioned officers, private soldiers and marines; white distinguishes the French; red marks the Spaniard; black the Prussian and Austrian, green the Russian, &c. . . . (French) . . . officers were not permitted to wear a cockade, unless they were regimentally dressed; and, singular as it may appear, the officers and men belonging to a certain number of old regiments in the Prussian service did not wear any mark in their hats. In England, the cockade is worn, in and out of regimentals, by every species of military character. Indeed it is so generally abused, that almost every prostitute, who can afford to keep a man or boy, trims his hat with it.*

COATEE, a short coat about as long as present-day jackets, just covering the buttocks. The length of a coat, by contrast, usually extended to just above the knee. When provided with facings, coats and coatees were known as regimentals.

COEHORN (Also Cohorn), a small light mortar.

COLICHEMARDE, a long thrusting sword with a blade which is broad near the hilt but narrows rapidly. Later models usually had a triangular blade.

COLORS, the flags or standards of an infantry regiment.

CONTINENTAL ARMY, military forces in the pay and service of the Continental Congress.

CORNET, in the military history of the moderns, the third commissioned officer in a troop of horse or dragoons, subordinate to the captain and lieutenants, equivalent to the ensign amongst the foot. His duty is to carry the standard, near the centre of the front rank of the squadron.

*This definition is from Charles James' *An Universal Military Dictionary*, London: T. Egerton, 1816.

129

CORPS, any body of forces, destined to act together under one commander.

CRAVAT, a cloth worn about the neck, usually over the shirt. Black was accepted as the most practical color. The cravat was later replaced by the stock.

CRAVAT (Cravate), the streamers in the national color or colors flown at the pike head of a color or standard.

CYPHER (Cipher), in the British Army, the initials of the sovereign, used as ornamentation on various plates, buckles, buttons, drums, etc. A regimental device was often added to the cypher.

D

DIMITY (Dimothy), a fine cotton material, often with a velvet-like finish.

DIRK, a kind of dagger used by the Highlanders in Scotland, which they generally wear stuck in their belts.

DOLMAN, the short coat worn by hussars; a short, snug jacket without tails, often laced across the front.

DRAGOONS, (Dragons, Fr.) in military affairs, are a kind of horseman, or cavalry, who serve both on horseback and foot; being always ready on every emergency, as being able to keep pace with the horse, and to do infantry duty. In battle or on attacks, they generally fight sword in hand after the first fire.

DRESSED, a means of preparing leather equivalent to the present day definition for "tanned."

DUFFLE, (Duffil), a coarse, woolen cloth.

DURHAM BOAT, a particular type of boat developed on the Delaware River, 40 to 60 feet long, 8 feet wide, and 2 feet deep. These boats were double-ended, fitted with keels for stability, and could be propelled by oar, pole, sweep, or sail. A 4-man crew could handle such a craft. Used by Washington during his Trenton Operations.

E

ENSIGN, in the military art, a banner, under which the soldiers are ranged according to the different regiments they belong to.

ENSIGN, or ensign-bearer, is an officer who carries the colours, being the lowest commissioned officer in a company of foot, subordinate to the captain and lieutenant.

EPAULETTES, military marks of distinction, which are worn upon the shoulders commissioned and warrant officers. Those for the (British) sergeants and rank and file of the colours of the facing with a narrow yellow or white tape round it, and worsted fringe; those for the officers are made gold or silver lace, with rich fringe and bullions. They are badges of distinction, worn on one or both shoulders. Rank of field grade officers was designated by two epaulettes. Company grade officers wore only one eaulette: captains on the right shoulder, sub-

alterns on the left shoulder. In the American service, silver epaulettes were worn by infantry and cavalry officers, gold by the artillery.

ESPONTOON (Esponton or Spontoon), Fr. a sort of half pike. On the 10th of May, 1690, it was ordered by the French government that every esponton, or half pike should be 8 feet in length. The colonels of corps as well as the captains of companies always used them in action. The officers of the British army were formerly provided with this weapon. . . .

F

FACINGS, lapels, cuffs, collar, and turnbacks of skirts covered or "faced" with a different color than the coat itself. The colors used often indicated regimental or corps designation. It can be surmised that the original facings were linings of the coat, exposed when the lapels and skirts of the coat were turned back in warm weather.

FEILIDH BEAG (Also Filidh beag, felie-beg, feile-beag, and philabeg), see LITTLE KILT.

FIELD OFFICER (or Field Grade Officer), a major, lieutenant colonel, or colonel.

FIRELOCK (fusil, Fr.) an instrument of modern warfare, so called from producing fire of itself, by the action of the flint and steel. The arms carried by a foot soldier. The [British] private soldier familiarly calls his firelock brown bess; although the term is little applicable to the weapon, considering that it is absurdly polished in almost every regiment in the British army. This practice not only gives unnecessary trouble to the soldier, but ultimately injures the piece; especially when the ramrod is used to give a high polish. Firelocks were formerly 3 feet 8 inches in the barrel, and weighed 14 lb.; at present the length of the barrel is from 3 feet 3 inches to 3 feet 6 inches, and the weight of the piece only 12 lb. The typical "firelock" of this period was a smoothbore, flintlock musket, caliber .69 to .75.

FUSIL (Fuzil, fusee, fuzee), A light musket.

FUSILEERS, in the British service, are soldiers armed like the rest of the infantry, with this difference only, that their musquets are shorter and lighter than those of the battalion and the grenadiers. They wear caps which are somewhat less in point of height, than common grenadier caps.

G

GAITERS, a sort of spatter-dashes, usually made of cloth, and are either long, as reaching to the knee, or short, as only reaching above the ancle; the latter are termed half-gaiters.

GORGET, a crescent-shaped piece of metal worn by an officer on duty. The gorget was the last relic of armor once worn by the knight and originally was the neck-piece upon which the cuirass or front armor rested. When the cuirass was discontinued, the gorget was suspended from the neck by ribbons and worn as a mark of rank.

GRENADIER or GRANADIER, a foot soldier, armed with firelock, bayonet, and in some services with a hanger; grenadiers carry, besides their arms, a cartridge box that will hold 36 rounds. They are clothed differently from the rest of the battalion they belong to, by wearing a high cap, fronted with a plate of brass, on which the king's arms is generally represented, &c. and a piece of fringed or tufted cloth upon their shoulders, called a wing: in some armies they have more pay than a common soldier. They are always the tallest and stoutest men, consequently the first upon all attacks. Every battalion of foot has generally a company of grenadiers belonging to it, which takes the right of the battalion.

GUNNER, in the artillery, the enlisted man responsible for aiming a cannon; in this period, had the approximate rank of private first class.

H

HACKLE, a small feather plume, worn in the hat.

HALF-THICKS, thin, comparatively light material.

HANGER, a short, rather heavy, cutting sword with a curbed blade; generally an infantry weapon.

HALBERD (Halbert), a weapon formerly carried by sergeants of foot and artillery. It is a sort of spear, the shaft of which is about 5 feet long, generally made of ash. Its head is armed with a steel point edged on both sides. Besides this point which is in line with the shaft, there is a cross piece of iron, flat and turned down at one end, but not very sharp, so that it serves equally to cut down or thrust with.

HALF GAITERS, see GAITERS.

HAVERSACK, a bag, usually of canvas or heavy linen, used in the field for carrying rations. Soldiers usually carried the bag over their right shoulder so that it rode their left hip and thus did not interfere with the cartridge box.

HUSSAR, a light cavalryman of the type originally developed in Hungary, famed for dash and showy uniforms.

J

JACKET, a term synonymous with "waistcoat" or "vest"; also a short coat with sleeves.

JAEGER, (also jäger) a German rifleman.

JEANS, twilled cotton cloth.

K

KILT, see LITTLE KILT.

KNAPSACK, a pack, sometimes made of cowhide with the hair left on the outside, or covered with fur. The usual American knapsack was made of heavy canvas, varnished to make it waterproof.

KURZGEWHER, a variety of espontoon with a fancifully shaped head; carried by noncommissioned officers in some German regiments.

L

LACE, flat braid used for trimming lapels, cuffs, and other portions of the uniform. The basic British lace was white; most regiments added a distinctive pattern of lines or "worms" in contrasting colors. Officers' lace was gold or silver matching the color of their buttons.

LAPELS (Lappels, lapells), the turned-back upper part of a coat or waistcoat. Lapels were usually worn buttoned back in warm weather allowing the distinctive color of their lining or "facings" to be clearly visible. In cold weather, lapels could be buttoned across the chest for warmth.

LEGION, During the Revolution, a legion was a force of battalion or regimental size, consisting of both infantry and cavalry. Occasionally, a small detachment of light artillery was added. Such organizations were much used for irregular warfare. Following the Revolution, the United States Army was organized on a legionary basis.

LIGHT HORSE, all mounted soldiers, that are lightly armed and accoutred for active and desultory service, may be considered under this term. Thus light dragoons, fencible cavalry, mounted yeomanry, &c. are, strictly speaking, light horse.

LINSTOCK (Also termed porte-feu, boute-feu, and portfire), an artilleryman's implement; a staff approximately 3 feet long with a forked iron head to hold a slow match; used to fire a gun.

LITTLE KILT, a kilt similar to those of modern design, developed about 1725 to replace the "Belted Plaid." It has a variety of Gaelic spellings including *philbeg, feilidh, felie-beg,* and *feile-beag.*

M

MATROSSES are properly assistants, being soldiers in the royal regiment of artillery, and next to the gunner; they assist in loading, firing, and spunging the great guns. They carry firelocks, and march along with the guns and store wagons, both as a guard and to give their assistance on every emergency.

MITASSES, Canadian leggings, adapted from Indian dress.

MUSKET (or musquet), the most serviceable and commodious firearm used by the army. It carries a ball of 29 to 2 pounds [Ed. note: 29 balls weighed 2 lbs.] Its length is 3 feet 6 inches from the muzzle to the pan. See FIRELOCK.

MUSKETEERS, during this general period, infantry men of the battalion companies.

MUSTER, in a military sense, a review of troops under arms, to see if they be complete, and in good order; to take an account of their numbers, the condition they are in, viewing their arms and accoutrements, &c. This word is derived from the French montrer, *to shew. At a muster, every man must be properly clothed and accoutred, &c. and answer to his name.*

N

NANKEEN (Nankin), a cotton cloth, usually yellowish-brown in color.

O

OSNABRIGS (Osnaburg, Ozenbrig), a German-type linen; also a heavy canvas sacking.

OVERALLS (Overhauls), loose trousers, sometimes worn over breeches and stockings, hence their name. In the American army, "overall" came to be long trousers, cut to strap under the instep and to fit snugly around the top of the shoe. The overall thus did duty as both trousers and leggings.

P

PATCHED BALL, a bullet (normally a rifle ball) which was wrapped with a scrap, or patch, of greased cloth to assure a snug fit and easy loading. This technique was brought to North America from Germany.

PATCH BOX, the small compartment in the stock of the rifle which contained greased patches used to seat a bullet. The patch box was covered by a hinged cover, usually of brass.

PELISSE, the short overcoat worn by hussars in full dress or cold weather.

PINCHBECK, imitation gold, made of an alloy of zinc and copper.

PIONEER (Also called a "carpenter"), picked soldiers who marched at the head of the column to clear away obstacles. Most infantry regiments had a detachment of three to six pioneers, equipped with heavy canvas or leather aprons, axes, saws, pick axes, and shovels.

PORTFIRE, see LINSTOCK.

PORTMANTEAU, leather case, carried behind the cantle on the saddle to hold a horseman's cloak and other articles. Often called a "valise."

PROVINCIALS, certain bodies of troops which were raised in America, during the contest with the natives, for the royal cause.

R

REGIMENT, a term applied to any body of troops, which, if cavalry consist of one or more squadrons, commanded by a colonel; and, if infantry, one or more battalions, each commanded in the same manner. The squadrons in cavalry regiments are divided, sometimes into six, and sometimes into nine troops. The battalions of British infantry are generally divided into ten companies, two of which are called the flanks; one on
the right consisting of grenadiers, and another on the left formed of light troops. There is not, however, any established rule on this head; as both cavalry and infantry regiments differ according to the exigencies of the service in time of war, or the principles of economy in time of peace.

RIFLE (Rifled gun, rifled piece, rifled barrel), Fr. A fire-arm which has lines, or exiguous canals, within its barrel, that run in a vermicular direction, and are more or less numerous, or more indented, according to the fancy of the artificer . . . by giving the balls a stronger turn, or spin, it enables them to maintain their flight with accuracy at considerable distances.

RIFLEMEN, experienced marksmen, armed with rifles. they formed the most formidable enemies during the war in America, being posted along the American ranks, and behind hedges &c. for the purpose of picking off the British officers; many of whom fell by the rifle in our contest with that country. . . . This has been called a murderous practice, and some persons have questioned how far it ought to be admitted in civilized warfare; but is not war itself a murdreous practice?

ROUND HAT, a hat with a low crown and narrow brim, usually of civilian styling.

ROYAL REGIMENTS, select British regiments of foot were awarded the additional title of "royal." These alone, with the Guards and the Regiment of Invalids, had the right to wear blue facings. In 1768, there was 10 royal regiments out of 70 regiments of foot. While this award was normally given for outstanding service, in some cases —as for example, the Royal Americans — it seems to have been given merely to stimulate recruiting.

RUSSIA DUCK, a fine, bleached linen canvas.

S

SABRETACHE (Sabre-Tasche), from the German sable, sabre, and tasche, pocket. An appointment or part of accoutrement which has been adopted amongst us for the imaginary use and convenience of dragoon officers. It consists of a pocket which is suspended from the sword belt on the left side, by three slings to correspond with the belt. It is usually of oblong shape scolloped at the bottom, with a device in the center, and a broad lace round the edge.

SCHABRAQUE (Shabraque), the name given the original Hungarian saddle cloth. Adopted by the British to cover a saddle, the cloth developed into an ornamental trapping.

SHAKO (Chako, Chakot), the type cap developed by the Austrians and adopted by the British during the latter part of the 18th century. Originally cylindrical and of a "stovepipe" design, the cap developed and was modified into many shapes.

SHALOON, a loosely-woven wool cloth, often twilled on both sides.

SLOW MATCH, a heavy, loosely-spun cord, boiled in lees of old wine. It burned slowly and was used to fire cannon. See LINSTOCK.

SMALLCLOTHES, uniform garments other than coats or coatees. These consisted of waistcoats, vests, breeches, overalls, and trousers.

SPATTERDASHES, a kind of covering for the legs of soldiers, made of cloth, or coarse linen waxed over, and buttoned tight; by which the wet is kept off; now called long gaiters.

SQUADRON, the cavalry equivalent of a battalion.

SPONTOON, see ESPONTOON.

SPORRAN, originally a leather pouch or wallet suspended from the waist belt. This was used because there were no pockets in the kilt. The modern sporran is an ornamental pouch rather than a practical accoutrement.

STANDARDS, the flags of a cavalry regiment.

STOCK, the whole of the wooden part of a musket or pistol.

STOCK (Col. Fr.), a part of an officer's dress, which consists generally of black silk or velvet, and is worn round the neck instead of a neckcloth. The soldier's stock is of black ribbed leather, and is part of his small mounting. Red stocks were formerly worn in the guards; they are still so in some Prussian regiments.

STROUD, a coarse, woolen cloth much used in bartering with the Indians; used for blankets and rough clothing.

SURTOUT, Fr., a great coat. We also use the word surtout to signify the outward garment of man, generally however one coat over another.

SWANSKIN, a thick twilled flannel with a downy surface.

T

TRICORNE (Tricorn), a 3-cornered cocked hat.

TROOP, a cavalry unit which was the equivalent of an infantry company.

V

VALISE, see PORTMANTEAU.

VENTPICK (or simply "pick"), an instrument attached to the cartridge box belt and used to free the touch hole of burned powder about every fifth shot. A vent pick was also a similar instrument used by a gunner to break open the powder bag by thrusting the pick down the vent or touch hole of an artillery piece.

W

WAISTCOAT, the garment worn under the coat. Also known as a vest. Generally, the waistcoat had no sleeves although a few sleeved varieties are known.

WATCHCOAT, a heavy overcoat, so called because it was issued to a sentry "on watch."

WINGS, crescent-shaped pieces of cloth sewn on the shoulder of the uniform coat. These were characteristic of the flank companies and musicians.

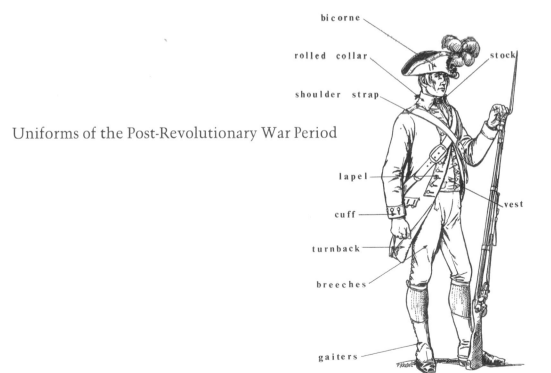

Uniforms of the Post-Revolutionary War Period

Index

140